THE HUNTED
WHALE

Also by James McGuane

HEART OF OAK

THE HUNTED
WHALE

JAMES McGUANE

W. W. Norton & Company
NEW YORK · LONDON

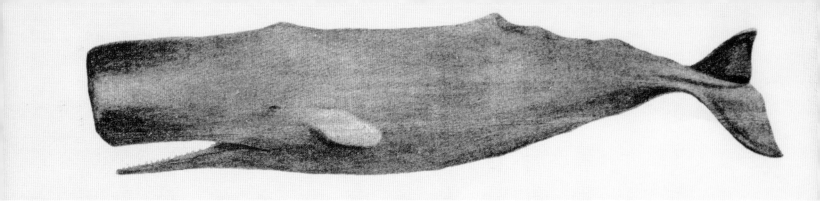

For information about permission to reproduce selections from this book,
write to Permissions, W. W. Norton & Company, Inc., 500 Fifth Avenue, New York, NY 10110

For information about special discounts for bulk purchases, please contact
W. W. Norton Special Sales at specialsales@wwnorton.com or 800-233-4830

Manufacturing by Shenzhen Donnelley Printing Co., Ltd.
Book design by Chin-Yee Lai
Production manager: Devon Zahn
Digital production director: Sue Carlson
Digital production: Joe Lops and Rebecca Caine
Composition: Adrian Kitzinger

Library of Congress Cataloging-in-Publication Data

McGuane, James P.
The hunted whale / James McGuane. — First edition.
    pages cm
Includes bibliographical references.
ISBN 978-0-393-06912-9 (hardcover)
1. Whaling—United States—History.
2. Whaling—United States—History—Pictorial works.
I. Title.
SH383.2M43 2013
639.2'8—dc23
                        2013009414

W. W. Norton & Company, Inc.
500 Fifth Avenue, New York, N.Y. 10110
www.wwnorton.com

W. W. Norton & Company Ltd.
Castle House, 75/76 Wells Street, London W1T 3QT

1 2 3 4 5 6 7 8 9 0

FOR BROOKE AND HER SISTERS

CONTENTS

WHALESHIP *CHARLES W. MORGAN*
Mystic Seaport

ACKNOWLEDGMENTS

———————◆———————

The photographic documentary is an adventure that can only hope to succeed with the massive help and cooperation of collectors, curators, scholars, museum officials, librarians, friends and others too numerous to name.

NANTUCKET

The Nantucket Historical Association and the Nantucket Whaling Museum generously put all of their resources at my disposal. Ben Simons, Elizabeth Oldham and Bob Hellman have my sincere appreciation. Tony Dumitru, Richard Wolfe and Suzanne Duncan also helped and extended warm island hospitality.

CAPE COD

David Wright at the Wellfleet Historical Society Museum was an early supporter of my efforts. Likewise, Marcella Curry and Lucy Loomis at the Sturgis Library in Barnstable. Collectors and experts include Ryan Cooper, Dick and Edith Broderick and Richard Kahn. Mary Sicchio, archivist at the Falmouth Historical Society, generously shared her research with me. The Brewster Ladies Library assisted in my research. Jessica Knight at Homeport Restaurant provided access to her splendid model of the Whaleship Charles W. Morgan.

NEW BEDFORD

Thanks to James Russell, Jim Lopes, Mike Dyer and Stuart Frank at the New Bedford Whaling Museum. Volunteers at the National Park Service were kind and helpful, as was Kate Corkum at the Rotch-Jones-Duff House and Garden. Judy Downey provided insight into the importance to Yankee whaling of those men from the Azores and Cape Verde.

Dr. Michael Moore is a veterinarian, biologist and whale expert with a stance both at the New Bedford Whaling Museum and at the laboratories at the Woods Hole Oceanographic Institution. He contributed greatly to this project.

BOSTON

Special thanks to Thomas Putnam and curator Heather Joines at the John F. Kennedy Library and Museum for making it possible to photograph JFK's scrimshaw collection.

MYSTIC, CONNECTICUT

It was a distinct privilege to have Matthew Stackpole welcome me aboard the whaleship *Charles W. Morgan*. His knowledge of that ship (and whaling in general) is deep and wide. Mr. Dana Hewson and Louisa Watrous and the curators at the Mystic Seaport Museum have my gratitude.

SAG HARBOR

Zach Studenroth at the Sag Harbor Whaling Museum on the North Shore of Long Island in New York was helpful and supportive. Sumner and Gail Braunstein of nearby Southampton have my appreciation.

COLD SPRING HARBOR

Mariners rely on "local knowledge" when sailing in unfamiliar waters. Taking on a pilot or consulting with local watermen can keep you off the shoals and rocks.

Similarly, at an early stage of my documentary research, I was most fortunate to meet Mr. Paul DeOrsay. Paul was a bona fide "blue water sailor" long before he became director of the Cold Spring Harbor Whaling Museum. He's not a whaler, but has particular expertise on the subject of whaleboats. That museum has the finest example that I've seen. The lightweight, 30-foot craft—fully equipped—was a gift of Robert Cushman Murphy. Mr. DeOrsay, who is now Executive Director of Friends of the Bay (Oyster Bay), spent many patient hours with me as I photographed the boat. He also suggested that I read Murphy's *Logbook for Grace*. Long sections of Murphy's riveting accounts of life aboard the whaleship *Daisy* in 1912 are excerpted in this book.

Robert Cushman Murphy was a recent graduate of Brown University, trained as a naturalist specializing in bird studies. He was offered an opportunity by the American Museum of Natural History in New York to travel on a one-year whaling and sealing voyage to the waters of the Southern Ocean near Antarctica. As the New Bedford ship *Daisy* hunted for whales and seals, he was to collect bird specimens. He and his fiancée, Grace, decided to marry and have a brief honeymoon before he set out on the long separation. His scientific journal faithfully recounts his activity on each day of the voyage. In addition to this huge volume of academic work, he kept a meticulous diary of ordinary events to share with his wife. The material contained in these papers is both valuable and timeless. Murphy went on to join the American Museum of Natural History for a brilliant forty-four-year career.

Murphy was in an ideal position to record the waning days of American whale hunting. His clear scientific vision brings to mind earlier naturalists Charles Darwin and John James Audubon. After months aboard the *Daisy* he was given the opportunity to actually participate in a whale hunt. His account is recorded here in Chapter One. Other observations are quoted throughout this book.

Thirty-five years after he wrote them, in 1947, parts of these entries were published as *Logbook for Grace*. His granddaughter Eleanor Mathews has graciously permitted us to use selected accounts that deal with whaling. Her own book, *Ambassador to the Penguins: A Naturalist's Year Aboard a Yankee Whaleship*, published nearly a hundred years after his voyage, adds personal insights into her grandfather's work and puts the importance of his studies into perspective.

A number of friends pitched in on the dozens of shooting days where I needed extra help. I dare not call them assistants since most are established professionals. Thanks especially to Eddie Lynch, Naomi Stock, Bill Hoenk, Daleela Farina, Karl Peiler, Jason Nower, Emmanuel Alexandre, Jr., and my early photography and production mentor Minoru Ooka.

Thanks to the Hasselblad Camera Company, Carl Zeiss Optics, Phase One Digital, Capture One Software, Digital Transitions and Canon Camera.

Thanks to blacksmith Pete Olivia in Sutton, Alaska; Thanks to Robert Parker, blacksmith in Walton, New York; The Ships of the Sea Maritime Museum in Savannah, Georgia, and E. Shaver, Bookseller—also of Savannah; Joan Druett in New Zealand; The Wampanoag Indian Museum in Massachusetts. M. L. Baron in offshore Massachusetts lent his expertise with scrimshaw. Joe Thomas of Spinner Publications and the kind people at the Milicent Library in Fairhaven, Massachusetts, were helpful with research. Thanks to John Hardy in California; the Kauai Museum in Hawaii; Rainer Judd in Hudson, New York; Brigid Kavanagh in Park Slope, Brooklyn; Susan Olsen at Woodlawn Cemetery; Daphne Nichols and the Lord Howe Island Historical Society, New South Wales, Australia; Dr. Richard Nugent at the Georgia Aquarium; Marcy Carsey and Susan Baerwald at Just Folk Antiques in California; Meghan Tillett for her help with JFK Scrimshaw material.

Friends and family have been patient and supportive, including Trudy McGuane, Sheila, Katie, Meg and Jamie—Frank, Patty and Joey. William Marcato, Judith Blumert, Jon Beekman Harrison, Jason Blumberg, Don Alloway, Clare Gennario, Rick Maclennan, Jay O'Brien, Rita Ragone, Tom Aberg and Mark Rabiner, MD.

Most patient and most helpful has been my editor Starling Lawrence at W. W. Norton & Company. He has guided the creation of this complex project with a sure and even hand. I thank him. His able assistant Ryan Harrington also has my sincere thanks as do the rest of the Norton Team: Devon Zahn, Nancy Palmquist, Susan Sanfrey, Adrian Kitzinger, Sue Carlson and Joe Lops. Finally, my gratitude is extended to my friend and literary agent, William Clark.

MELVILLE GRAVESITE
Woodlawn Cemetery
BRONX, NEW YORK

Melville's shaded resting place is between his wife, Elizabeth Shaw Melville, and his second son, Stanwix. In Melville's mother's day (Maria Gansevoort Melville) it was known that the surrounding farmland once belonged to another early immigrant from Holland—Jonas Bronck.

The carving on Melville's headstone shows a tracery of vines, a sharpened scrivener's quill and a blank parchment scroll.

Some who know and appreciate the adventure of the blank (and filled) page have left a reminder of their visit—often a small stone.

THE HUNTED
WHALE

BRONZE HARPOONER AGAINST THE SKY

Town of New Bedford

This larger-than-life–sized sculpture in front of the Public Library commemorates New Bedford's whaling past. There is a polished-stone monument nearby that records the risk-it-all exhortation A DEAD WHALE OR A STOVE BOAT. It let every man know what was expected of him.

Chapter One

THE HUNT

The hunt is one of man's most ancient endeavors. One can barely imagine an early time when man was free from the daily need to find nutritious food or eliminate a dangerous predator. It's been posited that language itself grew out of the need for precise communication as men stalked and hunted prey.

Preparations for a whale hunt were meticulous. Veteran whalers, the shipowners and the one selected to be "master" of the vessel would map out a strategy. They would draw on secret wisdom collected from hundreds of prior ventures. The "grounds" to which they sailed were also a guarded secret. Experienced whalers, often villagers and kinsmen, were selected to fill the most important roles aboard the ship. Up to two-thirds of the remaining slots on the crew could be young men with no whaling experience at all. Quite frequently, these greenhorns had no shipboard skills of any kind!

Food, clothing, weapons, wooden barrel parts, spare sails and spars and supplies of every sort were stowed for the voyage. What lay ahead, for all, was a rough, cramped society completely cut off from the rest of the world. There are numerous accounts of long voyages where the anchor never dropped during a year (or more) of sailing. It was on-the-job training in the months it took to reach the preferred hunting grounds. A watch for whales was set at the very onset of the cruise. Although an encounter with the desired prey was unlikely at the early stages of the voyage, men were sent on watch to the small perches, high aloft. In time, the "greenies" became used to the dizzying heights and their eyes were trained to discern a faint spout on the distant horizon. From this spout sighting they might also come to know the species, gender, number, course and attitude of their potential quarry. Their initiation into the hunting team continued.

The captain and the mates kept their own sharp watch over the men. Those few who proved to be strong, quick and handy were chosen to pull an oar in the whaleboat on an actual hunt. No amount of training could truly prepare a landsman for what lay ahead. A total assault on his senses lay just across the waves from his tiny, tossing boat. There may have been prior "practice runs"—some resulting in a kill—but a 20-foot "blackfish" or pilot whale would seem tame when compared to their first battle with a sperm whale.

The command "lower away all boats" sent the four or five 30-foot boats over the ship's side in pursuit of sighted whales. Each boat had a six-man crew. The boatheader (either the ship's captain or one of the three mates) commanded the boat and steered from the stern position. The harpooner, more correctly called the boatsteerer, manned one of the five oars. At his elbow were two of the surgically sharp tools of his trade carefully fastened to over a quarter mile of the finest marine cordage. As his "chance" with the whale approaches he is commanded to ship his single oar, stand and take up the first of his "irons." In the tense drama that will unfold, the life of each of the six men is dependent on his fellow man. The simple contest between man and whale was diabolically joined by a third (and frequently deciding) factor: the sea.

The Yankee shipowners entrusted their vessel to a single man—the master—or ship's captain. He knew well what was expected of him. In turn, every man aboard would soon learn his will: If whales can be taken, "lower away" no matter what the sea conditions. The ideal striking distance was "wood to black skin"—virtually "beaching" themselves on the whale's back. The iron was never "thrown" but "planted" or "darted." The word "thrown" would seem to imply a certain lack of resolve—as if the men lacked the courage to get close and fasten to the beast properly. Once harpooned, the enormous whale lashed out with unimaginable agility. The boatheader barked out highly specific commands to the oarsmen, who must now, quite literally, row for their lives to avoid the snapping jaw and massive flukes that were capable of dashing their boat to splinters.

If one or both harpoons held fast, hours of drama often lay ahead. They could be pulled along, skipping over the wave tops faster than they had ever traveled in their lives. Gradually, as the whale exhausted every means to get free, the men pulled themselves alongside their captured prey. The boatheader deftly changed positions with the harpooner and readied himself to jab his deadly lance, time and again, into the whale's "life." When his work was done, the oarsmen were commanded to pull to a safer distance as the animal howled and thrashed through the torments of his death flurry. Finally, as their quarry quietly floated "fin out" on an acre of blood-red sea, the exhausted men lay back from their oar for a few moments' rest. Freshwater and hard ship's biscuit was their feast.

Murphy handled the paradox of being an erudite gentleman confined among a crew of tough (mostly) illiterate Portuguese islanders with aplomb. He appreciated their courage and respected their whaling skills. They, in turn, befriended him and often aided him in his scientific work. This was the "sunset" of traditional whaling. He certainly saw that the slaughter of giant mammals for their oil could not continue. Later in life he would prove to be one of the "leading lights" teaching respect for the planet, oceans and in the "save the whales" movement.

Additional biographical information on this naturalist and museum curator can be found in the acknowledgments at the front of this book.

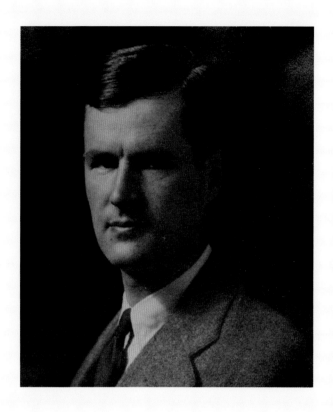

Excerpt from Logbook for Grace
by Robert Cushman Murphy (1887–1973)

MURPHY GOES WHALE HUNTING

October 10, 1912.

Evening.

This has been the most exciting day of my life. Even though the cabin lamp is a poor, dull flicker, I must pour my experiences on to paper while they are still fluid.

The morning broke gray and overcast, with a strong wind whipping the ocean. About eight o'clock a squall blew up, bringing a torrent of rain which was just at its height when a school of sperm whales rose a few ship's lengths to windward. The boats were at once cleared on the davits and all hands stood by. The rain presently slackened and the weather brightened enough for us to see at least two pods of whales spouting off our quarter, and others astern. When the order, "Lower away!" was shouted and echoed, I slid down into the mate's boat and took stroke oar, replacing a Dominican who remained with the shiptenders.

Seeing that the spouts were fast pulling to leeward, we stepped the mast, after reefing, for the wind was brisk and the sea choppy. As soon as the whales had sounded, indicating that they were foraging and not alarmed, we zigzagged and jibed to hold our headway, while we lashed the line tubs to the thwarts, poured sea water over the rope, and put all gear in order. Then the blue waif at the Daisy's masthead signaled "whales up" and gave direction. Mr. da Lomba pulled the tiller sharply; once more we jibed and made off before the wind, with the other two boats running abreast of us on either side. By this time it was raining a deluge again and we were drenched to the skin.

While we were bearing down toward the school, which was now steaming at the surface in preparation for the next dive, two good-sized bulls popped up unexpectedly just ahead and we were whisked upon them. The nearer of the pair crossed our bow and while its gray body glided along a little under water, Emiliano drove the iron into the whale's right side, just in front of the hump. As the beast leaped forward, his whole massive head breached above the surface and his flukes grazed the keel as he cleared us and dashed to windward, making the wet line groan when it tautened and began to rub around the loggerhead.

Sail was dropped, mast lowered, and rudder unshipped, while harpooner and mate changed ends, the latter forsaking the helm for the still more ticklish business of lancing.

Our whale's run was only for a short distance. Coming up with others of the school, he joined them and we could see him lying calmly at the surface. We four oarsmen now hauled line, the boatsteerer holding the turn around the loggerhead and coiling slack in the stern sheets as it was paid in. We pulled as hard and as fast as we could and, when we neared the whale, a strange sight was presented through a curtain of rain. Our whale lay wallowing, the harpoon shaft projecting from his blubbery back; beyond him were three or four half-grown calves. On the near side lay a second bull, belly up, his jaw and most of his head out of water, and our harpoon line caught between two of his teeth.

Mr. da Lomba gesticulated frantically for the other boats to come up, and we waited silently but in a shiver of impatience. Before Mr. Vincent's boat could arrive, the bull which had fouled our line, and which had probably been puzzled by the obstacle, allowed it to slip from its jaw. We then hauled up to the whale to which we were fast and, when the keel pressed his side, the mate drove in the long keen lance to the socket. Within the same instant the hump hove up, the great flukes reared in the air, our bow went down with a jerk, and we shipped a couple of barrels of water as the whale sounded.

Forty-barrel bull," said Mr. da Lomba.

Forty-barrel bull! I recalled what the Old Man had told me long before, that no big sperm whale is likely to make as much excitement for a boat's crew as a lusty forty-barrel bull, enjoying the most active period of his watery life.

For a quarter of an hour we bobbed about quietly within a small area, the line snubbed around the loggerhead, Emiliano expressing the sentiment of all good boat-steerers by slackening it as little as possible and only at the last moment of safety. Then the expected burst of vapor appeared to windward, the lopsided head began to seesaw with the pointed hump, and we shot ahead on our sleigh ride.

The sun broke through the louring clouds, thawing out our goose flesh while we strained at the line and gradually gained on our unwillingly harnessed beast. But the whale had been goaded to alertness, and the lance puncture had been too far aft to affect his staying powers. Before we attained even pitch-poling distance, he sounded again, jerked us about, carried us back two miles before the wind, and then, without rising to the surface, plunged deeper, tearing the smoking line after him and soon exhausting the two hundred fathoms in the large tub. When the contents of the small tub began to follow, we were in a quandary. But in the nick of time one of the other boats sailed alongside; we bent on borrowed line, and saved our forty barrels!

In the middle of all this fight into which I was putting all I had, I confess to a certain sympathy with the enemy. It seemed reasonable at least that after being pricked with the harpoon that still galled him, and pierced through with the horrible lance, the whale should wish to steer clear of us. This, however, was not at all the mate's idea of good form and fair play. Standing like an armed crusader in the bow of the boat, Long John da Lomba would scratch his head after the whale had sounded, and mutter, "I cain't understan' what make that animile so goddam shy!"

Our status, I thought from time to time, was that of the tin can on a dog's tail. We annoyed the whale, but were otherwise pretty helpless.

Time flies with a fighting whale on one's hands. The sun climbed to the zenith and its pleasant beams alternated with cold showers while we sped along over the rugged, white-capped Atlantic, wearing the skin off our palms in this yet undecided tug-of-war. The whale battled nobly for his life. He tried sounding, spinning, and running all ways with respect to the wind. At one time he was towing three whaleboats, besides two drogue tubs, one of which is alleged to offer as much resistance as four boats. Watching one of these tubs dragged through the water at high speed made me marvel that the single tiny harpoon was not ripped from its anchorage in the blubber.

During a midday tempest, the roughest period of our chase, the whale pulled us cross-seas through the troughs and crests so that combers slopped over the gunwales. It was then that we kicked off our oil-skin pants (I was the only man wearing shoes), so as to be unencumbered for swimming. Over and over again the bow was pulled completely under water, because a boatsteerer hates to slacken line. Three times we half swamped and had to let the whale steal line while all hands bailed; indeed, the piggins and our sou'westers were employed thus more or less continuously.

I have a dreamlike mental background for the day's play—the choppy, spumy water and the varying sky, the heliotrope Portuguese men-o-war that seemed to bob past us, the bright flying fish scared up, the inquisitive Mother Carey's chickens that fluttered astern; and, focus of it all, straight ahead, the rocking shiny back of our forty-barrel bull, with an impertinent little harpoon sticking there.

The brig appeared to shunt about magically, being now abeam, now close aboard off the bow, now nearly hull down astern. Fortunately, we were moving mostly in wide circles, for otherwise we should have been towed out of sight and would have had to cut line. Time and again we slacked away and tried to give another boat an opportunity to sail upon the brute and plant a second iron, but he was all wariness. When the boats came ever so softly within three or four lengths, he would kick up his big flukes and be gone. Mr. da Lomba eventually shot a bomb lance into the whale's back, but the rubber-feathered end of it broke off and went whizzing over the sea, while the cylinder failed to explode. Three more bombs from a shoulder gun were likewise vainly spent, and the mate concluded that the charges were watersoaked.

The turning point of the struggle came when the frantic whale once more fell in with a gam of his fellows. The calming influence of neighbors was soon apparent, for he allowed us to draw right toward him. We pulled ourselves through an acre of sperm whales, big bulls that we might have touched with oars, cows at arms' length, and tiny calves, ten or twelve feet long, with huge remoras clinging to their flanks. Such company lay unconcernedly awash all about us, but we paid it scant attention because it is quite sufficient to be fast to one sperm whale at a time.

"Shush, easy, easy boys," whispered Mr. da Lomba; "trim the boat; don't shift your quids [chaw tobacco]."

We hauled softly along the length of another whale and, when our line was as short as a dog leash, the mate braced his thigh in the clumsy cleat, raised his long powerful arms, and buried the five-foot shank of the lance in blubber and flesh. The tortured whale quivered and sank. We peered tensely over the side for his dark hulk, knowing that the sounding would be brief and that he might rise beneath us. The mate pounded and pried the twisted lance shaft into a semblance of straightness.

"Stern all!" Up came the whale under our keel. While we just avoided capsizing, the lance struck home twice or thrice again through the froth before the whale got under way on another lap of his race. Then everything was repeated. Once more we were drenched. Again we bailed and hauled and slackened and hauled and bailed.

Finally, the second officer's boat, which had been back to the brig, transferred to us a case of dry bombs. Late in the afternoon, when we once more entered a group of whales, the crucial opportunity was seized. A bomb was shot into the brute's lungs where it exploded with a muffled crack. In his leap, he half filled our boat with water for the last time, but he no longer had breath to sound. His spout, formerly so thin and white, reflecting tiny rainbows in the rays of the low sun, now became first pink and then crimson and gouted.

"His chimney's afire!" said Mr. da Lomba, with a heartless chuckle.

Mr. Almeida's boat closed in with ours. Lances were thrust between the whale's ribs, held there, and churned, until the creature went into his ghastly flurry, all the while belching squids from his gullet until we floated in a slimy pool of their remains.

He died and turned fin out after giving us nine thrilling hours. We chopped a hole through one of his flukes, attached a line, and rested, weary but content, munching hard bread, drinking fresh water, and awaiting the arrival of the distant brig which, happily, was then to windward. After all the bluster of the day, the sun set in a calm sky. Mars, burning red, followed closely on the same track, and was hanging like a lamp on the waters when the *Daisy* bore down and gathered us in.

ONE TOOTH, THREE VIEWS
Nantucket Whaling Museum

The view on the lower left shows animated hunting activity. Of the three whales visible, the one in the foreground has upset the whaleboat. In the background, to the far right, a sperm whale is "fast" and the boat is alongside ready for the kill. The oars point to the sky and a tiny figure with a lance is in the bow, nearest the whale. After the *coup de grâce*, the oarsmen would be commanded: "stern all"—to pull to a safe distance as the whale flittered on the surface in its circular death flurry.

The before-and-after scenario is continued in the horizontal view at the upper left. The starboard whaleboat is hanging in its davits and a "blanket piece" is being stripped from the whale carcass chained alongside. The artist uses the bottom surface of the tooth to name the ship as the *Rose* of Nantucket.

ENGRAVING, *SPERM WHALING—THE CHASE*

***THE SPERMACETI WHALE
OF THE SOUTHERN OCEAN***
***Engraved Illustration from* The
Natural History of the Whale**
EDINBURGH, 1837

This fanciful engraving from 1837
shows the hunting of a sperm whale.
The scale of the whaleboat to the
whale is incorrectly depicted. If
it were a 60-foot whale, a 30-foot
whaleboat would be half its length.
The angle of approach and the desirable attitude of "wood to black skin"
are accurate. The whale floats too
high in the water.

Fore—Whales are up.

Main—Whales to windward.

Misen [*sic*]—Whales to leeward.

Peak—Come to, or towards, the ship.

Fore & Peak—More whales in sight.

Fore & Main—Whales ahead.

Fore & Misen—A boat fast.

Main & Misen—Whales astern.

Misen & Peak—Boats far enough.

Main & Peak—More to the right.

Main, Misen & Peak—More to the left.

½ Mast Peak   One boat come on board.

All three mast heads—All come on board.

It was not unusual for a whaling captain's wife to accompany him on a voyage. Mary Chipman Lawrence sailed with her husband Samuel aboard the whaler *Addison* on an extended voyage from 1856 to 1860. Their daughter Minnie, who was five years old at the onset of the cruise, came along as well. Mary took an active, administrative role in the day-to-day affairs of the ship. She kept a detailed journal of daily activities as well.

Researchers found this single sheet folded neatly into one of Mrs. Lawrence's "account" books. It sets forth a coded arrangement of signal flags to be flown high in the rigging so as to be seen by the boats that had been lowered in pursuit of whales. Other whalers were frequently on the same grounds, and it was desirable to direct the activity of distant boats from the mother ship without letting competitors know your tactics.

DAVIT SUPPORTING A WHALEBOAT

New Bedford Whaling Museum

This is a detail showing a davit. A pair of these brackets suspended a whaleboat over the side of the mother ship so that it could be quickly lowered to pursue whales. Up to five whaleboats might be so arranged on a good-sized whaler. The hook at the end of the fall tackle grasped an iron eyebolt on the whaleboat. The crew slid down the lines after the boat was afloat. The mate (or captain) could assume his place in the boat and be lowered. A returning whaleboat often weighed a lot more than it did when it was lowered. Wet whale line, an injured man or a few inches of water would put extra strain on the light cedar craft.

The New Bedford Whaling Museum boasts the "world's largest ship model." The equipment shown here is from that half-scale model, the *Lagoda*.

WAIF—MARKING FLAG FOR A KILLED WHALE
Gosnold Support Center
Nantucket Historical Association

This is nothing more than a rectangle of fabric and a rod of wood a bit thicker and longer than a broomstick. A thin kerf has been sawn through the pole to allow the fabric to be wedged in between. A series of small nails pinches it all back together. The other end has been sharpened to a rough point and notched with a barb.

When a whale was killed, it typically rolled to one side. It was said to be "fin out." If the hunting was good and other whales were to be had, the kill was marked with a waif. This flag helped later in locating the prize, which was barely buoyant and showed little above the rolling seas.

SHIP MODEL, *JOHN COGGESHALL*

Martha's Vineyard Museum

John Coggeshall, sailing from Newport, Rhode Island.

Chapter Two

THE SHIP

The American whaleship, perhaps because of its notoriously violent and bloody harvest, has been maligned as a slovenly sailing craft. An unbiased view would reveal that as a working craft it is almost ideal. Once it was finally perfected in the early 1800s, its design changed very little over subsequent decades. The changes that *were* made addressed the new strains and stresses, which were brought on as the seasonal hunt for whales took them to previously forbidding and icebound waters.

It's tempting to apply the twentieth-century architectural notion that "form ever follows function" when critically surveying a whaleship. Unadorned Yankee practicality is what was really behind its design. It was said that the New England shipyards "built them by the mile and cut them off as needed." The truth in that statement is that they indeed had a bluff bow and slab sides. Those ships, large and small, that were built specifically to go whaling, share similar qualities. The bark *Charles W. Morgan* that was launched from New Bedford, Massachusetts, in 1841 now resides at Mystic Seaport in Connecticut. Her stout construction has provided her with a long life. To walk her decks helps us to understand the whaling life.

The captain, or ship's master, ruled supreme from his quarters in the stern of the vessel. He was, no doubt, a man of substance onshore, so every attempt was made to provide him with a modicum of comfort. The physical space of his quarters, cramped as it may have been, was at least ten times the size of the cabin occupied by the first mate. There was a skylight above his sitting room, or saloon, which provided him with instant communication with the helmsman who was steering the ship. The compass card was visible even at night so that he might note the course being steered. If need be, he could bound up the few steps in the companionway and be on the main deck. When settled below, he had a comfortable couch, or settee, a separate dining room, and a sleeping chamber with a gimbaled bed to counteract the ship as she heeled to one side. He had a washstand, a toilet, a galley of sorts, and closets, cupboards and cabinets full of his private store of foods and other perquisites.

Just forward of the captain's quarters on the *Charles W. Morgan* is the mate's "cabin." Although its proportions are little more than that of a broom closet, virtually every other man on the ship would envy it. It had privacy, a chart table and a shelf where the ship's log was kept—one of his important duties. A small oil lamp on the bulkhead would light his navigational charts—his other critical duty. Moving forward, there were smaller and more cramped quarters for the other ratings such as the second and third mates, cooper, cook, steward and harpooners. One's value and esteem at any given point was indicated by the size and location of one's berth. A demotion might find one all the way forward in the vessel in the cramped, stinking, squalid fo'c's'le where the new men were billeted. Rude wooden shelves acted as bunks and were stacked lower, middle and upper. Another man's feet would likely rest just inches from your head. The crew was divided into two watches so each bunk would have two successive occupants.

The uppermost, or weather, deck was the principal theater of operations on a whaleship. In the blink of an eye, whatever task was at hand could be efficiently put aside so that more pressing needs could be met. A prime example would be the command to prepare to lower boats in pursuit of whales. A precise choreography of men loading the last of the critical gear into the whaleboats that were hanging "at the ready" from their davits over the side of the ship was well rehearsed. Often, as little as a minute's time was all that would be needed to see one or more boats with their complement of six men pulling at the oars in pursuit of whales.

The varied tasks that took place on the tight confines of the upper deck were legion. The ship had three giant masts with a labyrinth of attendant lines and sails. The mainmast had distinct lines and tackles for all of the brute heavy lifting required of the ship as massive carcasses were worked. All hands would labor at the winches and windlass to rip long sections of the dense blubber from the dead whale floating along the starboard side so that it could be lowered through the yawning hold in the deck into the cavernous blubber room below. If whales were being taken, room was needed to store the oily fat. Only after this "cutting-in" operation was completed could the command be given to start the fires under the processing kettles.

The brick "tryworks" was a strange sight on the deck of a sailing ship. Its presence might cause shivers to marine architects and shipwrights. It added great extra weight high above the waterline and employed open flame on a wooden ship. It was essentially a barbeque pit about 12 feet by 6 feet and rose to about chest height. The firebox below heated (at least) two open kettles above—each having a capacity of about 250 gallons. The area was often called the "goose pen." Livestock of all kinds was frequently fenced in there. The cooper often set up temporary workbenches there for not only his barrel and cask fabrication but also for general carpentry and blacksmithing tasks that were asked of him. It was not obvious from viewing the ship from the outside, but she was built with closely spaced ribs, and her hull had tremendous "hoop strength" to stiffen her and make her equal to the heavy industry she routinely carried out.

The *Charles W. Morgan* made thirty-seven voyages over a working life of about eighty years. She was a home to the men who worked her. She was a launching platform for the small boats that actually took the whales, and she was a processing and refining factory. She was a floating, cavernous warehouse for all the barrels of oil she had harvested.

PANBONE WITH SCRIMSHAW SCENE
Nantucket Whaling Museum

This is a very large panbone from a sperm whale. Although it's no more than ¼ inch thick in most places, it strongly supports the whale's toothed lower jaw. It has a close grain and a density unlike most of the other structural bones in the whale's skeleton. Here it has been polished like ivory and decorated with a panorama of whaling activity.

    The water around the ship to the right has been stained red to document the cutting-in operation. A blanket piece of blubber has been stripped from the carcass and can be seen hanging from the main-mast. There is a cartoonist's sense of suspended animation among the activities of the small whaleboats. The artist was obviously respected for his skill to have been provided with such a vast canvas.

FORWARD HAWSEHOLES

Main Deck, Charles W. Morgan

Mystic Seaport

Hawseholes, pronounced *HAWzulls*, are iron reinforcements meant to allow heavy lines of rope or steel or the chunky anchor chain to pass smoothly through the hull.

In lowering the huge anchor, the chain is "flaked out" on the deck, and an end is passed through one of the holes and shackled to the ring on the anchor, which is secured in place along the bow. Lashings are cut that allow the anchor to drop into the water. The chain fairly screams through the iron fitting. Retrieving the anchor can be a slow backbreaking job for the several men straining at the windlass, which is just a few feet away. Link by link the chain is drawn in. In time the men will have to muscle the weight of the vertical length of chain and the weight of the anchor, *and* overcome the "grab" that the anchor's flukes have on the seafloor.

MODEL WHALESHIP

Three-Quarter View of
Starboard Side (top)
Straight-On View of
Larboard Side (bottom)
Nantucket Whaling Museum

This is quite an accurate view of a whaleship, as she would look before "bending on" sails and heading for the whaling grounds. We see on the starboard view that there are just two whaleboats hanging in the davits. The "cutting stage" is folded inward until whales are brought alongside for processing. The flat covering just aft of the foremast protects the kettles and tryworks from the elements. The cover will, of course, be removed as the blubber is boiled.

The larboard view shows three whaleboats.

Optimism was high as a whaleship left on a cruise, but having scores of tight (but empty) casks ready for filling was not the way things happened. The owners did have the foresight to pack foodstuffs, clothing, blankets and other sundry stores and supplies in casks that could hold oil once their initial purpose had been served. The cooper would maintain a steady pace as he fashioned the raw materials (staves, heads and hoops) into strong, leakproof barrels and casks.

The anvil shown here is called a "devil." It's small when compared with those that would be found at the village smithy. The "horn" at the front is round and lends itself to forming flat straps of iron into barrel hoops and setting rivets. The sharp-edged chisel pointing upward is a "hardie." Heated (and sometimes cold) metal strapping can be positioned over it and tapped with a hammer to shear it off cleanly. The "tang" of the hardie can be tapped upward to release it from the square hole. The devil itself has a long tang, which is wedged into a stump of wood shown with an iron collar around the top. The whole tool was quite portable and probably saw a variety of use around the ship.

The cooper was a valued position on a whaleship. He would be offered attractive compensation. His "lay" would be on a par with the second and third mates and the boatsteerers. His quarters would also reflect his status among the crew.

TILLER TO THE WHALESHIP *LIMA* AND HANGING SIGN
Nantucket Historical Association

The stout tiller used for steering the ship is almost upstaged by the grand door hinges at the Gosnold Support Center, home to much of the "reserve collection" of the Nantucket Historical Association. It can be seen that the tiller and sign once worked together as a hanging display. The ship, apparently, had a working life of thirty-two years. The Pacific and South Sea fisheries began in the late 1780s. The name *Lima* suggests the coastal Peruvian city that became well known to whalemen.

It probably took more than a single man to steer a vessel through the legendary waters around Cape Horn with this heavy wooden tiller attached directly to a large wooden rudder. The very thought of such an attempt without a ship's wheel is chilling.

The *Lima* was a 160-ton schooner built at Pembroke, Massachusetts, in 1804—although the sign dates her first voyage at six years later. She had several successful voyages to the newly discovered whaling grounds off the west coast of South America—west of Chile and Peru. She had seven voyages where she took sperm oil exclusively. On the homebound leg of her final voyage, the *Lima* was boarded by pirates, who plundered the vessel.

STARBOARD HAWSEHOLES

Main Deck, Charles W. Morgan

Mystic Seaport

Bringing a killed whale alongside first involved making secure attachment points at his head and at his tail. A line or chain was fastened to the whale and passed through one of these holes (also called hawse pipes) from the outside and drawn tightly. A similar line was drawn through a hole toward the stern. Adjustments could be made so that the butchering always took place directly beneath the cutting stage, which is in the waist of the ship on the starboard side, canted out over the water.

HALF-HULL MODEL OF A WHALESHIP

Nantucket Historical Association

Hundreds and hundreds of whaleships came out of New England and other shipyards, but very little material exists in the way of architectural drawings or models such as the one we see here. The boxy shape of the bow was a conscious design decision that favored storage space and a rock-steady stance in the water over hull speed.

STERN VIEW OF THE *CHARLES W. MORGAN*
Mystic Seaport

The whaleship *Charles W. Morgan* is currently undergoing a thorough restoration at the shipyard in her current home port of Mystic, Connecticut. She has been pulled out of the water and rests in specially built cribbing. Her masts and much of her other heavy equipment have been removed for the multiyear project. Her current disarray offers us a unique opportunity to look back in time at whaleship construction. An impressive set of highly technological tools has been used to assay, measure and calibrate the needed repairs. Certainly, power tools were not available when her keel was laid in the 1840s, but she will go back into the water much as she did back then.

The Gulf Coast disaster that was Hurricane Katrina yielded some "live oak" timber that met the requirements of the restoration. Several massive baulks were harvested from fallen trees. Their bark was spray-painted with the letter *M* to note that they were to be trucked northeast to the sawmill at Mystic Seaport.

BITT
Main Deck, Charles W. Morgan
Mystic Seaport

A thousand different loads and cargoes came and went through the main hatch for storage below. The bitt was an all-purpose post for temporarily "tying off" a load. It was integral to the basic structure of the ship. The single piece of wood is pierced with an iron rod. The post tapers slightly at the top and is capped with lead sheeting to weatherproof it.

ANKLE BUSTER—SHIP'S WHEEL MECHANISM
Main Deck, Charles W. Morgan
Mystic Seaport

The helmsman steered from this position, which is all the way aft on the main deck. His feet necessarily straddled the square post that traversed the short distance behind him to the enormous wooden rudder. As he made corrections in the ship's course, the entire wheel would swing through its short arc, one way or the other. A rogue wave or other sea smashing against the rudder would send this wheel mechanism through its arc unexpectedly—hence the colorful nickname.

There is a light wooden canopy over the helmsman's head, which offers a bit of protection from the elements. A small window in this roof allows him to check the trim of the sails. Just forward of the wheel there is a glass skylight built into the deck, which affords communication with the captain's quarters below.

WINDLASS LOCATION
Main Deck,
Charles W. Morgan
Mystic Seaport

The large wooden reel of the windlass has been removed, to facilitate the restoration project. Also called the spindle, this vital tool would ride in the bearing—the keyhole-shaped fitting shown here in the background, at the right. A matching bearing is located at the larboard side. The iron linkage to the pump handles is located just behind the large center post. A team of men faced each other and pumped opposing handles up and down to cause the windlass to turn. The wooden pawl is the thick plank, which is securely hinged so that it can drop into the next "tooth" on a gear that rings the center of the windlass reel. It assures that every incremental gain against the load is saved with no backwinding.

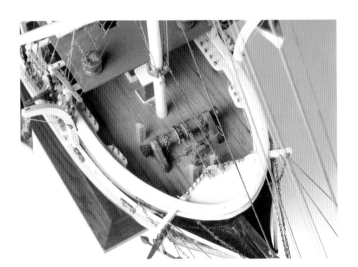

HIGH ANGLE VIEW OF WINDLASS
Model of the Charles W. Morgan
Homeport Restaurant
ORLEANS, MASSACHUSETTS

The finely detailed model shows the powerful (man powered) tool as it will appear when the Morgan restoration project is completed.

BULWARKS REPAIR

Forward on the Main Deck, Charles W. Morgan
Mystic Seaport

The curve of the bow and the outward slope of the bulwarks can be seen. The bulwarks acted as a fence around much of the ship to keep men and material from being lost overboard. It sheltered the men from the wind a bit and added a buffer as the fires raged under the trypots. The deck was frequently greasy and slippery, so the protection afforded by the high bulwarks was important.

The light planks that have been removed show that the ribs behind them are both massive and tightly spaced. These ribs most likely date from the original construction in 1841. If they fail to pass the inspection that is in progress, they will be replaced.

HULL REPAIRS AT THE "TURN OF THE BILGE," TWO VIEWS
Whaleship Charles W. Morgan
Mystic Seaport

The wide view faces the bow with the right side, obviously, to starboard. Many of the curved ribs (futtocks) have been replaced or had new sections added. The steel I-beam overhead lends precision to the restoration but will be removed at its completion. Numbers have been assigned to key components and are tagged both inside and outside the vessel. The system helps the shipwrights to keep track of their progress and also to determine the precise location for fasteners. Workers have jury-rigged a box fan in the overhead for a bit of breeze.

Returning from a successful, or "greasy," voyage this lower hold would be packed with casks of whale oil.

The second, close-up view is in the same attitude. This is the tight space very near the bow. When the *Morgan* was launched, whales were hunted mostly in temperate waters. Over her long working life whales were pursued in higher and higher latitudes. From the Japan Grounds (and points north) to the New Zealand Grounds (and points south) whaleships often found themselves in ice fields. The sturdy wooden crisscross bracing seen here was added well after her launch to strengthen her for the assault of floating blocks of ice.

SALT SHELVES
SAWN REPLACEMENT TIMBERS
Lower Hold, Charles W. Morgan
Mystic Seaport

One picture here shows the old timbers that were revealed when the thin horizontal planks (called "ceiling") were removed. Closer inspection showed little wooden baffles wedged horizontally between the larger timbers. The white pieces of cardboard mark where each was located. It was determined that they were "salt shelves." Rock salt was apparently packed tightly between the verticals. The shelf kept the granules from all settling toward the bottom. By staying in place they acted to "pickle" the wood in the damp environment and prevent rot and decay. The second photo shows newly replaced timbers with shelves added at appropriate points. The spidery white line in the first picture was formerly stretched taut by workers as a "level line."

CAST-IRON PUMP HEADS
Main Deck, Charles W. Morgan
Mystic Seaport

A gang of crew members worked up-and-down pump handles (missing from the picture) to draw water from the bilges far below. The water would gush out with each stroke and run to scuppers, or drains, along the edge of the deck. The number of strokes per hour would be recorded in order to see if progress was being made. If the efforts were not sufficiently productive, the crew would hasten to locate and stop the leak.

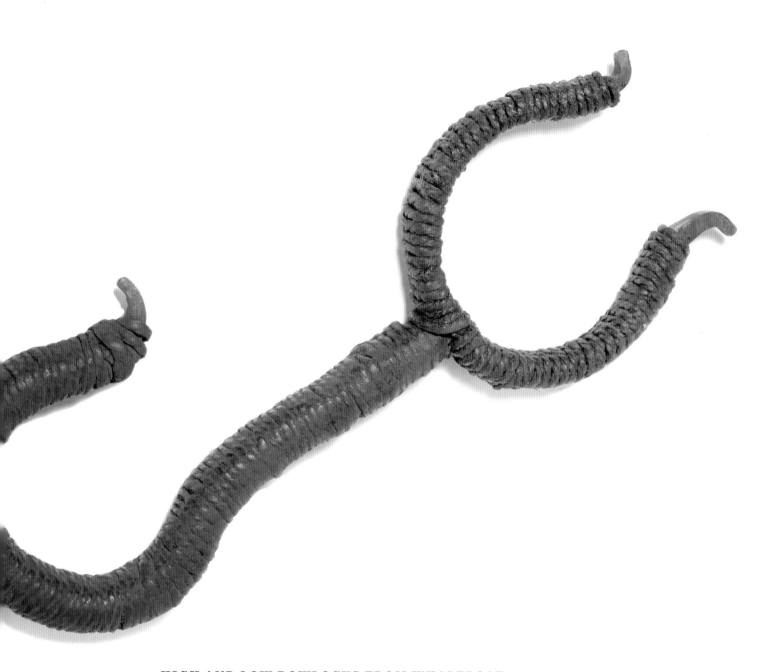

HIGH AND LOW ROWLOCKS FROM WHALEBOAT
Nantucket Historical Association

This curious piece is forged into a single piece of iron. The lower rowlock was for normal "pulling" (rowing) as the boat was muscled through the water. The upper rowlock was employed—when the boat was fast to a whale—to keep the long (inactive) "tub" oar from interfering or getting afoul of the whale line as the whale dragged the boat through the water. Both elevations of the rowlock were "served" with the light marline. This would act as chafing gear to keep the wooden oars from abrading into splinters as a dead whale was towed back to the ship, and, more important, it muffled the sound as a hunted whale was approached.

    The shank of the device is pierced with a small hole, which would allow the insertion of a pin, lanyard or other "keeper" device. That prevented the piece of hardware from bumping loose and going over the side.

SHIP FIGUREHEAD
New Bedford Whaling Museum

MELVILLE POEM
"THE STONE FLEET"
From His 1861 Published Piece:
Battle-Pieces and Aspects of
the War: Civil War Poems

Melville's *Moby-Dick* was published in 1851. Here, a decade later, the success he could today enjoy eluded him. He set out early in the American Civil War to record his firsthand experiences in a collection of poems: *Battle-Pieces and Aspects of the War*. One of these poems is "The Stone Fleet."

The war planners in the North bought a fleet of decrepit ships—many had been Nantucket and New Bedford whalers. They loaded them with rocks and rubble (hence the name Stone Fleet) and set out with the intention of scuttling them in such a way that they would impede shipping, mainly in the ports of Savannah, Georgia, and Charleston, South Carolina. The Confederacy would certainly look to receive supplies and war matériel through those ports. It proved to be a fool's errand. They were sunk in positions that could be avoided by vessels both large and small.

Melville, a bona fide whaler, does not hide his feelings of disdain. He calls the act "a pirate deed."

"The Stone Fleet," by Herman Melville

"An Old Sailor's Lament"

DECEMBER 1861

I have a feeling for those ships,
    Each worn and ancient one,
With great bluff bows, and broad in the beam;
    Ay, it was unkindly done.
        But so they serve the Obsolete—
        Even so, Stone Fleet!

You'll say I'm doting; do but think
    I scudded round the Horn in one—
The Tenedos, a glorious
    Good old craft as ever run—
        Sunk (how all unmeet!)
        With the Old Stone Fleet.

An India ship of fame was she,
    Spices and shawls and fans she bore;
A whaler when her wrinkles came—
    Turned off! till, spent and poor,
        Her bones were sold (escheat)!
        Ah! Stone Fleet.

Four were erst patrician keels
    (Names attest what families be),
The Kensington, and Richmond too,
    Leonidas, and Lee:
        But now they have their seat
        With the Old Stone Fleet.

To scuttle them—a pirate deed—
    Sack them, and dismast;
They sunk so slow, they died so hard,
    But gurgling dropped at last.
        Their ghosts in gales repeat
        Woe's us, Stone Fleet!

And all for naught. The waters pass—
    Currents will have their way;
Nature is nobody's ally; 'tis well;
    The harbor is bettered—will stay.
        A failure, and complete,
        Was your Old Stone Fleet.

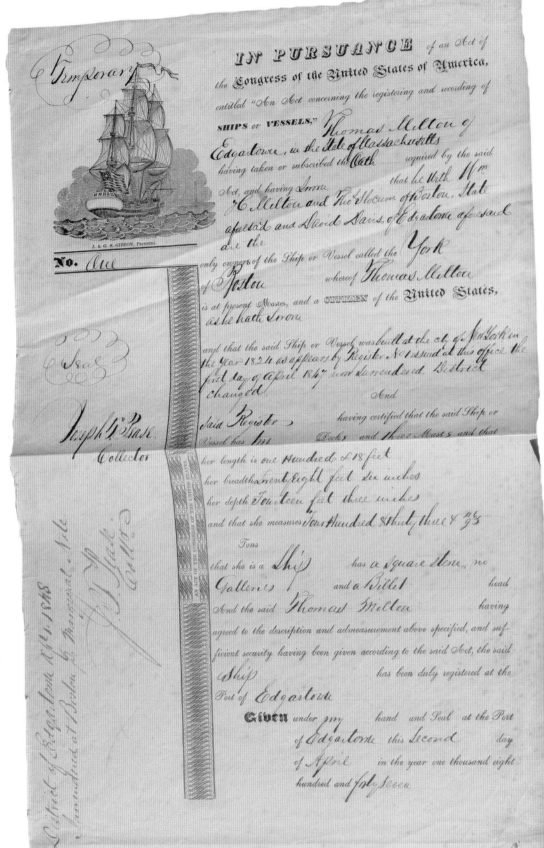

REGISTRATION FOR THE SHIP *YORK*
J. & G. S. Gideon, Printers
Martha's Vineyard Museum

At some point the U.S. Congress acted to require ship registration. Here, in 1847, Thomas Milton of Edgartown, Massachusetts, swears under oath as to the owners, sailing rig, dimensions, draft and general description of the ship *York*.

The blank registration form is finely engraved and employs a "security strip," presumably to deter counterfeiting. A little cloud-shaped balloon at the upper left indicates that the document is "temporary."

FIGUREHEAD FROM THE WHALESHIP
TAMERLANE
Private Collection of Ryan M. Cooper
YARMOUTHPORT, MASSACHUSETTS

The *Tamerlane* was built in Wiscasset, Maine, in 1824. Part of her ownership was in Savannah, Georgia. She spent her first twenty-five years in the cotton trade. In 1850 she was acquired by New Bedford owners who took advantage of her capacious holds and converted her into a whaleship.

Tamerlane was a dashing conqueror and ruler of the fourteenth century. The figurehead remained on the whaler until 1858 when it was replaced by a simple billet head—a carved scroll similar to the one we see here at Tamerlane's midriff.

**TWO WHALESHIP BELLS FROM
THE *OHIO* AND THE *PALLADIUM***
Private Collection of Ryan M. Cooper
YARMOUTHPORT, MASSACHUSETTS

The larger bell is from the whaleship *Ohio*. The ship was built for Nantucket owners in 1833. The bell itself was cast on the island of Nantucket. Edward Field had a foundry there. Written across the top of the bell is "E. Field Nantucket 1833." It measures 12 inches across at the mouth, a typical size.

The second is the watch bell. Typically, a whaleship had two bells. A large one was mounted forward near the fo'c's'le and a smaller one, the watch bell, near the helm. The helmsman would strike the bell to note the beginning of watches. The helmsman's signal would be immediately repeated by another man forward at the main bell. The forward bell would be used to announce the ship's presence in fog or darkness. It was also the fire alarm. On a warship (more so than on a whaler) the main bell would be used in Sunday divine services.

The ship *Palladium* was built in Salem, Massachusetts, in 1817. It became a whaler in 1820. It made whaling cruises from Boston and later from New London, Connecticut. Eventually, like many whaleships it made a one-way trip to San Francisco in 1849. Its final voyage carried men caught up in the frenzy of the gold rush. It ended its days as a store ship—tied up at the dock and used as a warehouse. It's believed to have been destroyed by fire in the 1850s.

There is some thought that the *Palladium* bell could have been cast at the Paul Revere Foundry. At the time the ship was built, the Revere Foundry was the only one in operation in the Boston-Salem area.

Mr. Ryan Cooper, of Cape Cod in Massachusetts, is a nautical scholar and collector. He comments: "The ship's bell is considered almost a spiritual thing with a ship. It's the heart and soul—and also the voice of the ship. In wreck-diving the bell is always the thing the divers most want. It's the most important artifact—if not the most valuable."

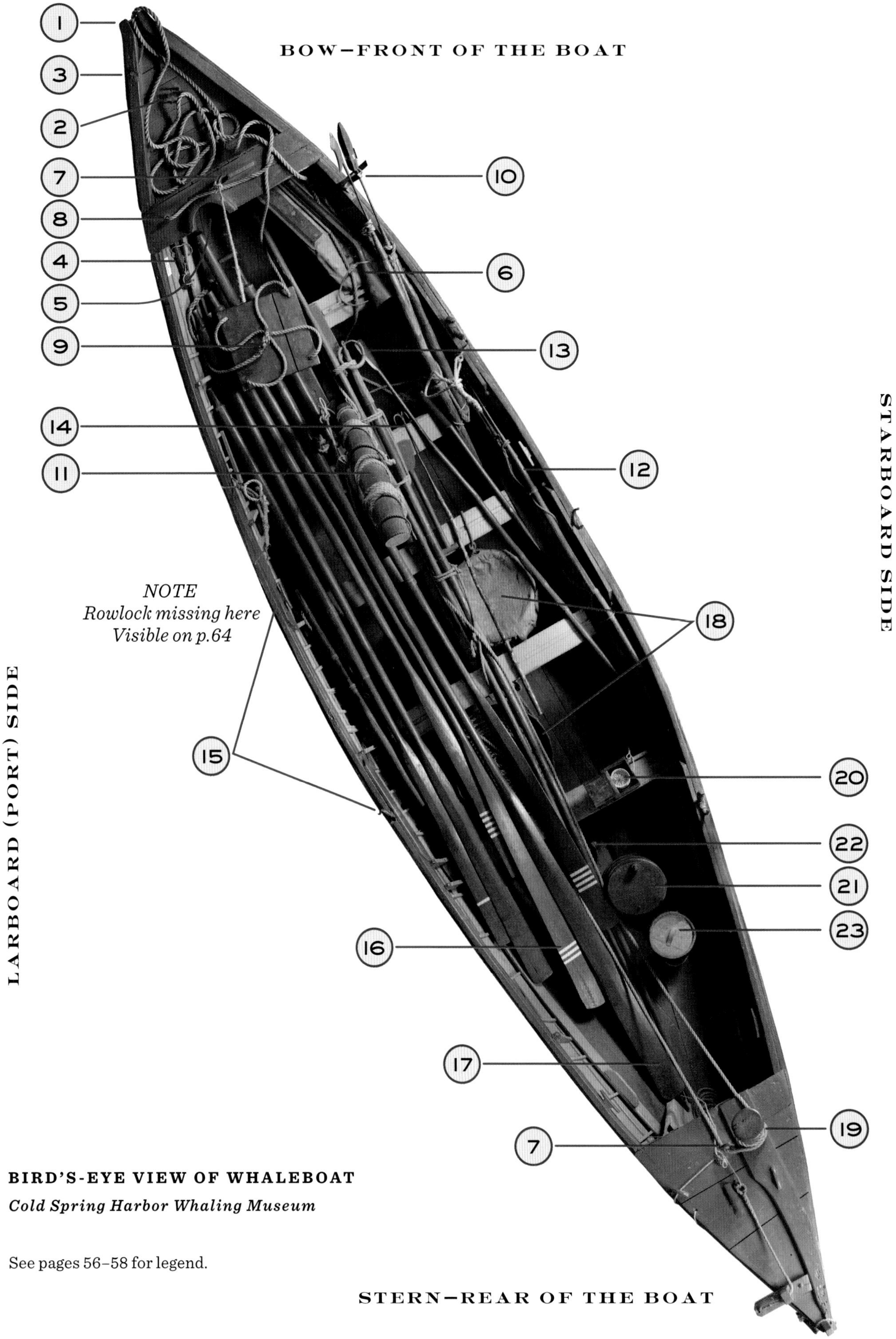

BOW—FRONT OF THE BOAT
STARBOARD SIDE
LARBOARD (PORT) SIDE
STERN—REAR OF THE BOAT
1
3
2
7
8
4
5
9
14
11
10
6
13
12
18
15
20
22
21
23
16
17
19
7
NOTE
Rowlock missing here
Visible on p.64

BIRD'S-EYE VIEW OF WHALEBOAT

Cold Spring Harbor Whaling Museum

See pages 56–58 for legend.

Chapter Three

THE WHALEBOAT

Much was expected of the 30-foot whaleboat suspended from davits over the side of the Yankee whaleship. Design and construction requirements were skillfully met in the late 1700s, and the whaleboat changed very little over the next one hundred years.

It was a lightweight craft of cedar lapstrake construction, a canoe-shaped "double-ender" that carried the hunting party of six men and a thousand pounds of gear. It could be propelled by oars, paddles or sail. The craft was expected to bring the men silently within touching distance of the whales. Once the first (and perhaps the second) "live iron" was darted into the now-enraged whale, the whaleboat was expected to be agile and responsive to the oars to avoid the instinctive moves of the whale's jaws and tail (flukes). Once clear of the initial violent thrash-

ings, it needed to be equal to the pounding ride across the water as the fleeing whale would frequently take the boat and men on the notorious "Nantucket sleigh ride."

The thrifty Quakers of Nantucket and New Bedford knew well the strains and stresses that would assault the whaleboat. Besides the hunting, it was often necessary to tow the captured whale's carcass back to the mother ship. That chore would be the equivalent of dragging the bodies of several bull elephants through the waves.

The whaleboat would be used to ferry passengers ashore, and to carry water casks, firewood, livestock and provisions of every sort back to the ship. The surf, especially in the South Pacific, could make for a forbidding and dangerous landfall. The whaleboat could navigate narrow coral reefs and float like a cork over the combing seas in the rare times it was necessary to put ashore. Once ashore, it was light enough to be pulled safely onto the land. A whaleship generally carried a spare boat or two and a good supply of cedar lumber. The cooper had the skills to build a replacement boat in a few days. A whaleboat (or the material to make one) was very desirable as "trade goods" at almost any port in the world.

Whaleboats were produced by the thousands at small yards throughout New England. They were simple and inexpensive. Being a true double-ender, the stem pieces and the stern pieces could be used interchangeably in whaleboat fabrication.

The mast and sail were also a picture of simplicity. Only a single pulley, or "sheave," was needed to hoist or lower the canvas. Each of the five rowers would pull a single long oar made of ash wood. They sat on the thwart on the far side—away from the rowlock, to generate maximum leverage. The men were well trained and could follow the crisp commands of the boatheader, who stood in the stern and managed the "sweep," the long steering oar. The whaleboat was swift and responsive. A short round stub of wood, the loggerhead (or king post) jutted up from a miniature "deck" at the very stern of the boat. On getting fast to a whale, the whale line was looped a time or two around the post and then directed forward to the "bow chock." The mate in the stern could then "snub" the line and increase the load that the whale must pull, thus tiring him. The ability of the craft to safely absorb such strains is a marvel of marine architecture.

LEGEND TO BIRD'S-EYE VIEW OF WHALEBOAT (PAGE 54)

1 The only thing forward of this bow chock is the "sharp end" of the whale line—the primary and secondary harpoons. There is about 30 feet of line, or warp, between the two.

2 This is a cluster of spare wooden pegs. (A close-up view can be seen on page 63.) One is fitted into the bow chock to keep the line flowing smoothly forward as the harpooned whale "takes line." Young harpooners, when ashore, wore a peg like these as a lapel decoration and as a visible sign of success at hunting.

3 The killing lance is a surgically sharp blade on a long, thin iron rod. The rod can bend quite easily. This notch has been placed at just the right angle so that the boatheader can use it for a bit of leverage to straighten bends and kinks that the thrashing whale may have caused.

4 A sharp hatchet was always kept here. If the whale line became fouled or suddenly posed a danger, the hatchet could be used to chop the line and release the whale. Scars on the small "deck" indicate that it was used on several occasions.

5 The "clumsy cleat" was a notch provided for the harpooner to steady himself as he darted his two irons. His left thigh fit here as he delivered each weapon with his right arm. A left-handed harpooner could have his whaleboat notched for his right thigh.

6 Inevitably, gunpowder came into use in whaling. This shoulder-fired gun delivered a long, cigar-shaped, exploding projectile called a bomb lance. When shot into a vital point of the whale's anatomy, death could be

almost immediate. Well into the twentieth century such devices were frequently carried—but seldom used. Thrifty Yankees considered each projectile exorbitantly expensive. Damp gunpowder caused frequent misfires. The weapon stood as a "last resort" against a whale that posed a threat to the boat and crew.

7 There are forged iron rings "through-bolted" at both the bow and the stern. The boat is raised and lowered on the davits by having the falls attach at these points.

8 Kicking strap. This simple rope "preventer" will have the whale line passing under it when hunting. When fast to a whale, that line is as taut and straight as a banjo string. If either the whale or the boat turns or veers sharply, the line can be wrenched from its intended path. This short rope is intended to keep the line from slicing aft.

9 This drogue (often pronounced *drug*) could be fastened to the line that is fast to a whale. It's really just a flat assembly of sturdy planks. Its intended purpose is to check the whale's speed and tire him. Shore whalers had similar ploys. They would attach logs, barrels, floats and other devices. Inuit hunters would sometimes attach inflated seal bladders.

10 Live irons. Two harpoons are shown at the ready. One is shown in its protective scabbard. The two (joined by a warp of rope) went over the side at each attempt at a whale. They might be retrieved for future attempts if the whale was not struck. A few spares were usually carried. A "crutch" was fitted into the gunwales to rest the irons and keep the sharp edges from harm's way.

11 The mast in this top-down view of the whaleboat has been truncated photographically. It has been *literally* truncated where it resides at the Cold Spring Harbor Whaling Museum on Long Island in New York because the roof of the building is not tall enough to handle its full length. As shown, the mast is "stepped" (set in the sailing position). It was usually precisely stowed at the men's feet, along the centerline, with sail, halyards and other rigging. Some crews could step the mast and raise the sail in about a minute.

12 The lance had a razor-sharp head, a long iron shaft, and was permanently affixed to a long wooden pole. It was well over half the length of the boat and was necessarily stowed safely out of the way (covered with a scabbard) until the boatheader came forward, exchanging places with the boatsteerer to administer the *coup de grâce* to the exhausted whale.

13 The "boat spade" was a paddle-shaped piece of steel mounted on a short pole. The forward edge was kept very sharp. When a dead whale was brought alongside the whaleboat, the spade would be used to gouge a hole through the tough tissue near the flukes. This was usually the attachment point for a towrope.

14 This grapnel is a treble hook fitted with a slender wooden handle. It could be used to grab anything floating near the whaleboat.

15 There were three rowlocks on the starboard side of the whaleboat and just two on the larboard side. When the boatsteerer was commanded to ship his oar and take up his harpoon, there would be two men "pulling" on each side.

16 Each man had an assigned position and pulled a single oar. The oars were of different lengths and marked with a stripe for easy identification.

17 The sweep was the longest oar and had a second grip near the handle. The sweep could be used to steer the rowed boat and, as its name suggests, could be wagged back and forth to propel the boat forward.

18 Line tubs. Ropeworks and cordage companies would position whale line called tow line in the trade, as one of their premier products. They would boast of its strength and suppleness and assure that it was made with

the finest in materials and workmanship. The larger tub held a length of line of between 200 and 225 fathoms (a fathom is 6 feet). The end of the line is pigtailed up from the bottom so the second tub's line may be added. The smaller tub usually held about 75 fathoms of line. *(Note: Uncovered line tubs visible on page 65.)*

19 Loggerhead. The loggerhead was a stout wooden post that was wedged securely in the stern of a whaleboat. It was positioned off of the centerline, nearer the starboard side. The whale line would be directed aft and given a couple of turns around the post before being sent forward. The boatheader could apply tension to the line to slow its travel and cause the whale to work harder towing the boat. He would have a rude canvas mitt to protect his hand.

20 Compass box. The whaleboat would frequently find itself some distance from the ship. Darkness, fog, snow or rain could set in and isolate the six men in their small craft. They relied on the compass and their canny navigation skills to survive.

21 Lantern keg. The lantern keg was a tightly sealed container that held some vital (and welcome) short-term survival supplies. When it was broken open, the men would find a tinderbox for striking fire, a lantern, candles, hard ship's biscuit, pipes and tobacco. The boatheader could use it as a reward after a successful kill.

22 The piggin was a wooden scoop used for bailing the whaleboat. The wind, waves and the general business of handling oars and whale line made bailing out the boat a constant chore. The piggin, essentially a wooden bucket, could also be used to splash quantities of seawater into the whaleboat. The men's sou'wester (oilcloth) head covering would also be used for bailing. When fast to a whale that was taking line, it was the tub oarsman's assigned job to keep the whale line and the loggerhead post wet. Heat buildup could degrade the whale line or even allow the snubbing post to catch fire.

23 Water keg. Pulling at oars in pursuit only meant more pulling when a whale had been taken. A hot meal would greet the men only when they were back aboard the ship. Water was vital to the men as they toiled with little protection from the elements.

Extra gear. Each whaleboat had to be self-sufficient and store everything necessary to hunt and retrieve the killed whale. It carried paddles, spare irons and lances, a boat hook, a box of bomb lances, special gear for towing a whale, and a marker flag (waif) on a wooden handle to let the ship know the position of the dead whale.

WHALEBOAT:

The leverage of whaleboat oars is extremely powerful because each rower sits at the end of his thwart farthest from his oarlock. Midship oar, with its oarlock on the starboard gunwale, is the longest—18 feet. Bow and tub oars, respectively afore and aft of the midship oar, are shorter and of identical length. They both rest on the port gunwale. Harpooneer and after (or stroke) oars, nearest bow and stern and both starboard, are the shortest of all and likewise identical. Thus one long and two shorts to starboard work against two of medium length to port. And how our boats skim and fly when they race all abreast toward the brig!

MODEL WHALEBOAT
Martha's Vineyard Museum

The scale and accuracy of this model are quite good. The exploded view shows us the two basic harpoons and a spare. Next to them we see the killing lance and a spare. Two oars are shown in their rowlocks. The remaining three, as well as the sweep oar, are to the left. The sail, mast and other spars form a bundle at the top. (Frequently the mast was arranged in a "hinged tabernacle" that would allow it to be stepped quickly.) The rudder, with tiller attached, is shown at the far left. It was secured on the outside of the hull on the stern quarter when the boat was not rigged for sailing.

   The model clearly shows the whale line leading aft from the line tub, with one full "turn" around the loggerhead post. Thus, the boatheader can adjust the tension as the line travels forward and is threaded through the bow chocks and (presumably) onto a fleeing, harpooned whale.

MASTHEAD SIGNALS FOR WHALEBOATS

Whaling Bark J. P. West

Martha's Vineyard Museum

There was clearly no standard arrangement for communication between a whaleship and her boats. Here, Captain Hall has outlined thirteen different schemes. The final two communicate simple facts: "Fast Boat" indicates that one of the boats was successfully engaged with a live whale. "Stoven Boat" broadcasts the fact that those on the ship can see that one of their boats has been damaged or wrecked. The officer on each of the other boats would react accordingly.

SIGNALS FOR WHALING

Martha's Vineyard Museum

Here, all involved had only nine signals to remember. The third, "Whales 4 points weather bow," is a clever device to use the ship as a giant "pointer." Steering the ship into the correct attitude and effecting the "Flying jib run up and down" sends the urgent message: "Over there! Over there!" Equally graphic and hard to miss is the emergency signal for "Boats stove"—"Colors at all three mastheads."

Signals for Whaling

Whales up.
Colors at mainmast or foremast head
Whales ahead.
Flying jib run up and down
Whales 4 points weather bow.
Weather clew of fore top gallant sail hauled up.
Whales weather beam.
Weather clew of main top gallant sail hauled
Whales astern.
Head of Spanker hauled down.
Whales between Ship and Boats.
Top gallant sails lowered.
Boats stove.
Colors at all three mastheads.
Boats aboard.
Colors at mizzen Peak.
Nearest boat come aboard.
Colors half mast at mizzen Peak.

WHALEBOAT

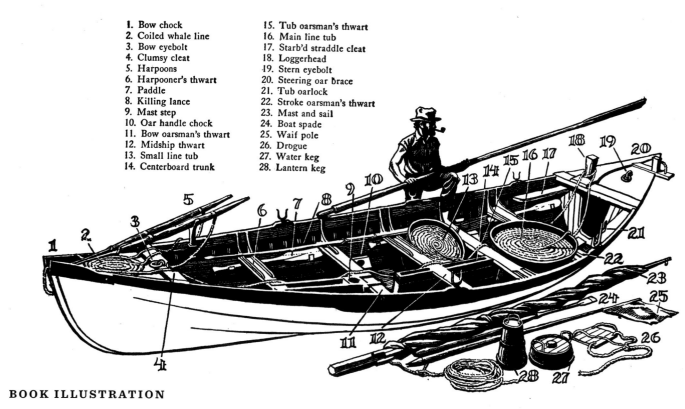

1. Bow chock
2. Coiled whale line
3. Bow eyebolt
4. Clumsy cleat
5. Harpoons
6. Harpooner's thwart
7. Paddle
8. Killing lance
9. Mast step
10. Oar handle chock
11. Bow oarsman's thwart
12. Midship thwart
13. Small line tub
14. Centerboard trunk
15. Tub oarsman's thwart
16. Main line tub
17. Starb'd straddle cleat
18. Loggerhead
19. Stern eyebolt
20. Steering oar brace
21. Tub oarlock
22. Stroke oarsman's thwart
23. Mast and sail
24. Boat spade
25. Waif pole
26. Drogue
27. Water keg
28. Lantern keg

BOOK ILLUSTRATION

An Exploded View of a Whaleboat and Supplies

Trained crews were sometimes capable of lowering the 30-foot boat from her davits in less than a minute. Most equipment was already in place.

SPARE WOODEN PEGS IN BOW OF WHALEBOAT

Cold Spring Harbor Whaling Museum

These little pegs, about the size of a golf tee, were wedged into the "bow chock" to keep the whale line from popping out of its groove after the harpooner had gotten fast to a whale.

At home, a harpooner would often wear one in his lapel (as one would wear a boutonniere) to let everyone see that he had actually taken a whale.

WHALEBOAT FROM THE WHALESHIP DAISY
Cold Spring Harbor Whaling Museum

MASTHEAD LOOKOUT HOOPS
Cold Spring Harbor Whaling Museum

Melville and many other whaling writers
recount the endless hours they have spent
in the masthead hoops on the lookout for
whales. The lookout usually has a 360-degree
view of a featureless ocean. The movement
of the ship over the water causes the masts to
trace lazy circles in the sky.

The iron hoops are "served" with light
line to ease chafing against the occupants.

Chapter Four

THE CREW

Each man on an outbound whaling cruise would have his name and "quality" entered in the ship's papers—or more correctly the Whaleman's Shipping Paper. The quality would delineate his job description (if he had one) or in most cases he would simply be called a green hand.

The critical jobs on the crew would be filled only after carefully examining a man's references from prior voyages. Records were scrupulously kept by the shipowners of each cruise. A man would sign or indicate with his mark that he had been paid—after the final tally of his share was done. He would be given a letter of discharge indicating that his employment on that vessel had ended. A black mark, or even faint praise from his superiors on an earlier cruise, could stop his whaling aspirations cold. Discipline problems, drunkenness, laziness or insubordination would be dealt with severely on a man's existing ship, and virtually preclude such future employment if it were noted in his work record.

The ship's **captain**, or master, reigned supreme once at sea. His certain responsibilities to his crew were outlined in the ship's papers, but harsh treatment somewhat short of actual criminal abuse was all too common.

Second in line of command was the **first mate**. This would be a trusted hand who had proven himself on earlier voyages. He presumably possessed many of the skills that might qualify him to command a vessel one day. If the captain was not aboard, was disabled or dead, the first mate assumed command of the ship.

There usually followed three additional "officers," the **second mate**, **third mate** and **fourth mate**. As their designations would suggest, they usually had less experience and were given lesser responsibility. The ship's papers, prepared as the vessel embarked on a cruise, also would list boatsteerers (harpooners), a cooper, a cook and often a steward. In every case, the man's "share" of the voyage—or "lay"—was precisely recorded. There was no fixed salary in compensation for any of the crew's labor. When the oil and whalebone were ultimately sold at market and all accounting was completed, each man would be paid the percentage that was recorded at the time of his hire (less expenses, of course).

Once the cruise was under way, new men were tested, watched and evaluated by their superiors with an eye to assigning the five vital oars on each of the hunting boats. On the proving ground of the open ocean the green hands' prospects could rise or fall. As the former landsmen acclimated themselves to their new shipboard duties, boats were often lowered to encounter a pod of blackfish, as whalemen called the pilot whale. Oar positions would be assigned and the boats would lower in pursuit. The mechanics and procedures of the hunt were the same, but the hazards (and the rewards) were considerably lessened. The blackfish were usually a manageable size (about 20 feet in length) for the hunters working from their 30-foot whaleboats. In time, on the prime whaling grounds, they would be attacking whales that were easily twice the length of their craft. The aptitude (and courage) that the men exhibited on these early forays would build muscle and sinew in the oarsmen that could win them a permanent spot on a hunting crew.

From the first day out of port, lookout watches were set to look for whales during daylight hours. There could be three or more hands braced in positions high aloft scanning the horizon for signs of whales. This tedious chore was assigned to the experienced men as well as the green hands on a fixed rotation.

The **boatsteerer**, the actual title of the harpooner, was a valued man, who was expected to hunt with courage and killer instincts. He could not falter in these traits a single time without running the risk of a humiliating demotion. There were any number of cocky young men on the ship who coveted this vital job.

The **cooper**, or barrel-maker, was expected to perform just a few functions aboard ship beyond his skill at seeing that the precious oil was secured without spills or leakage. The ship frequently sailed without a proper carpenter or blacksmith, and the cooper was called for any of the myriad repairs and maintenance chores on the ship and her boats. He was expected to work feverishly at the grinding wheel as the blubber was being stripped to keep the cutting spades and other edges razor-sharp.

The **cook** on a whaling vessel had a reputation for poor skills. Quite often he was asked to feed the men with a larder that was poorly stocked by the owners ashore. His was a never-ending challenge to provide the men with nutritious food that also tasted good. If his meals pleased the captain and if the men were served on time, he merely tolerated the friendly gibes from the crew.

The term "**seaman**" or "**able seaman**" is only occasionally seen on crew lists. Perhaps this means that a professional sailor felt it was beneath him to ship on a whaler. More likely, the owners preferred to rely on the mates to train raw recruits to "hand, reef and steer." The whaleship was never in much of a hurry and there was seldom any need to sail the ship aggressively. Once on suspected "whaling grounds," the ship merely dawdled along, hoping that whales would wander past. When whales were encountered, the ship was basically "hove to" with most of the key manpower out in the small boats hunting whales. Ideally, the ship was motionless after whales had been captured, as all hands were mustered for the butchering and boiling.

FO'C'S'LE COMPANIONWAY
Charles W. Morgan
Mystic Seaport

Fo'c's'le, of course, is a contraction for "forecastle" from a time when the prow of a ship may have resembled the armed parapet of a castle. One accepted pronunciation is *FOLKzull*. There are those who would suggest that it is a play on the word "foxhole."

This narrow passage is the only way the men could get in or out of their dark, confined den. It would seem luxurious, compared to that on some ships, as it has steep wooden steps instead of a mere rope ladder. The hatch could be covered in foul weather.

FO'C'S'LE, MEN'S QUARTERS
Charles W. Morgan
Mystic Seaport

This looks like a theatrical set. It requires a bit of imagination to feel what life was like here during the eighty-year working life of this vessel.

It was never this clean or this empty. The bunks are stacked three high. The bedding consisted of straw mattresses known to the men as a "donkey's breakfast." The solid wall at the back of each bunk is the ship's hull. When the ship was under way, one could feel and hear the bow pushing through the water. As you tumbled up for your four-hour work shift, your bedding would be used by another man as he came off watch. Tobacco was chewed or smoked in a pipe by most men (and boys). Rain, snow, blubber and soot were frequent sleeping companions. The sea chests anchored to the deck were the only real private space afforded a man. The chests also served for seating. A little whale oil burning in the lantern cast a bit of light.

ROTCH FAMILY HOME
New Bedford, Massachusetts

The mens' shipboard labors could pay handsome rewards for the ship owners and investors who remained safely on the shore. The Rotch family was a Nantucket whaling and merchant dynasty. In spite of the Quaker disdain for ostentation, this was once considered one of the finest homes in America.

IRON MANACLES
Martha's Vineyard Museum

The captain and the ship's officers were necessarily stern disciplinarians in dealing with the crew. Life in the "close quarters" shared by all on a vessel could lead to everything from petty disputes to murderous rage and near-mutiny. The captain ruled with absolute authority at sea. In extreme cases a man could be "put in irons" or otherwise restrained until he could be brought up on charges in the next port of call.

FRAMED OIL PAINTING
Captain Absalom Boston—Master Mariner
Nantucket Whaling Museum

For Absalom Boston's entire life, from his birth on Nantucket in 1785 until his death there in 1855, slavery was a fact of life in much of America. Although his father, Seneca Boston (also Nantucket born), had once been enslaved, Absalom was born a "free black." His mother, Thankful (Micah), was a Wampanoag Indian. Absalom was raised in a family that encouraged hard work, literacy, land ownership and business skill. His uncle (possibly his grandfather), Prince Boston, was an enslaved black whose master signed him on to what proved to be a successful whaling voyage. On his return, Prince refused to turn over his hard-earned "lay" (wages) to his "owner." He went to court and won not only his money—but his freedom. Later in life Absalom would also successfully use the courts to insist that his daughter, Phebe, not be excluded from Nantucket's municipal school.

Absalom himself went to sea as a young man and used the money he earned at whaling wisely. He was a homeowner at age twenty. Records show his numerous real estate and business transactions, including the granting of a permit to operate a "public house." The area of Nantucket known as Five Corners was the center of much of his activities.

The signature event in his whaling life was as master of the whaling schooner *The Industry*. The short six-month cruise was only a modest commercial success—the ship returned with just seventy barrels of oil. It was remarkable in that he sailed with an all-black crew and brought them all back safely. This was a bold venture at a time when "blackbirding" (illegal slave trading) was still a lucrative practice. The respect and affection that the men felt for their captain can be seen in this ditty written aboard the *Industry*:

Come all you noble colored tars
That plough the raging main
Come listen to my story boys
A thing that is quite strange

It was on the 12th of May my boys
Eighteen hundred and twenty two
A schooner from Nantucket boys
With all a colored crew

A F Boston was commander
And him we will obey
We took our anchor on our bow
Intent to go to sea
. . .

Here is health to Capt. Boston
His officers and crew
And if he gets another craft
To sea with him I'll go.

LAND-SHARK EMPLOYMENT CONTRACT

Martha's Vineyard Museum

"South Street" in the 1870s was a rough-and-tumble New York
City waterfront. Vessels and sailors of every sort "came and went."
The whaling center of New Bedford was 200 miles away and in
constant need of workingmen. Today, men such as J. Morison
of Whalemen's Headquarters would be known as "employment
agents"; at the time, they were generally known as "land sharks."

Their "prey" was any able young lad that they could entice
into the whale trade. Here, we would assume that a twenty-seven-
year-old skilled hand, a cooper, knew what he was signing and
what a whaling voyage entailed. A naïve green hand might sign on,
accept a dollar or two only to find himself committed to (eventually) repaying that, paying for his transport to New Bedford,
paying for food and lodging in New Bedford until he's billeted
aboard a departing whaleship and paying for the clothing and gear
required for his (often) multiyear voyage.

Mr. Morison's form says: "Voyages Settled." Since everyone
aboard is working for a lay, a share of the profits, Morison is
assured by the shipowners that settlement with *him* comes
before the man sees a penny. All too frequently, because of these
and other "advances," a man saw nothing from the settlement.

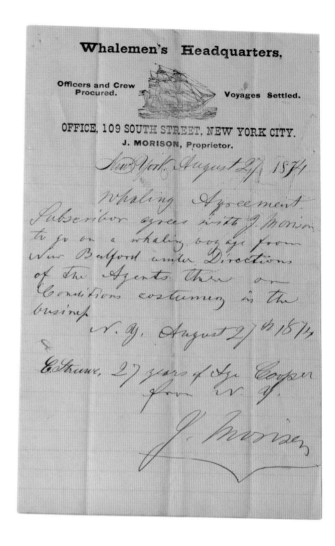

IRON-CLAD SHIPPING CONTRACT

Martha's Vineyard Museum

It's hard to discern *who* is agreeing to do *what* with *whom* according to this contract. Mr. Williams as
"Shipping Agent" includes himself (he uses the word "we" five times and the word "us" once) in
matters of clothing purchase, voyage on a ship (as yet unnamed), future "daily
wages," board and "any other expenses."

It's likely that Mr. Newman and
Mr. Dow would soon
learn the bitter lesson:
Some men rob you with
a gun—others with a
fountain pen.

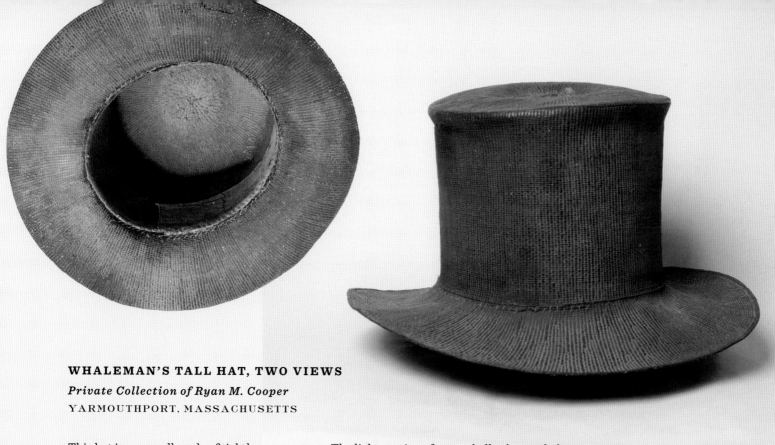

WHALEMAN'S TALL HAT, TWO VIEWS
Private Collection of Ryan M. Cooper
YARMOUTHPORT, MASSACHUSETTS

This hat is very well made of tightly woven straw. The light coating of tar or shellac has sealed it nicely.

WHALEMAN'S FLAT HAT, TWO VIEWS
Private Collection of Ryan M. Cooper
YARMOUTHPORT, MASSACHUSETTS

Around the globe, sperm whaling grounds were frequently found near the equator. A hat with a broad brim was an essential piece of a whaler's costume. You can see from the underside view that it's basically a straw hat that any farmer might own. For sea duty it has been covered with a light canvas fabric, which was then "water-proofed" with tar or shellac.

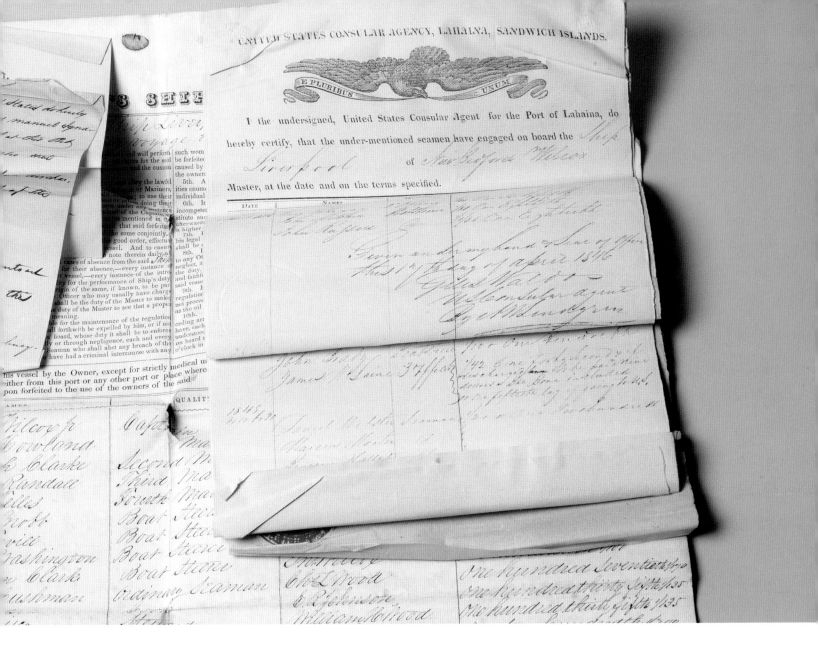

**WHALEMAN'S SHIPPING PAPER
FROM THE NEW BEDFORD SHIP *LIVERPOOL*, DETAIL**

Private Collection of Ryan M. Cooper

YARMOUTHPORT, MASSACHUSETTS

Upon arriving at each new port, the *Liverpool* would be asked to "show her papers." This "certified copy" (and other documents) would be produced from the safety of the captain's quarters. The packet of documents would get thicker and thicker as the ship got "additional stamps on her passport." It would provide a running record—where the voyage had begun and where the ship had been. The paper with the engraved eagle at the upper right is from the consular office in the Port of Lahaina in the Sandwich Islands (Hawaii). Lahaina became such an important center of Pacific whaling that it was known as "Little New Bedford."

The paragraph immediately above the crew list (readable on the facing page) warns: "No Distilled Spirituous Liquor will be put on board this vessel." Be he master, officer or seaman, the penalty was clearly spelled out: "his entire share of the voyage shall be thereupon forfeited."

WHALEMAN'S SHIPPING PAPER FROM THE NEW BEDFORD SHIP *LIVERPOOL*

Private Collection of Ryan M. Cooper

YARMOUTHPORT, MASSACHUSETTS

A large blank form titled "Whaleman's Shipping Paper" would probably have been available at any stationer's around New Bedford or Nantucket. A fresh one would be needed for every voyage.

When completed, it detailed the name of each member of the crew from the captain to the lowest ship's boy. It described the time each man signed on, his quality, that is to say carpenter, first officer, cooper, green hand, seaman, etc. There was an entry next to each man's information that proscribed his "share"—the percentage that he would be paid from the proceeds of a successful voyage. This voyage was to the "Pacific and Indian Ocean."

One of the entries lists a "George Washington—Boatsteerer." The name may be coincidental with that of the Founding Father or it could be something else. At the time, 1844, Africans, free blacks and, sometimes, runaway slaves found employment in whaling. As they set out on a new life on the high seas, they frequently were given, or adopted, patriotic names. The designation "boatsteerer" (actually, harpooner) and the generous "share" that he had agreed to would indicate that George Washington had proven himself on at least one previous voyage. Many New England shipowners were practical and thrifty Quakers. Their simple belief in the equality of all men put them in the vanguard as equal-opportunity employers.

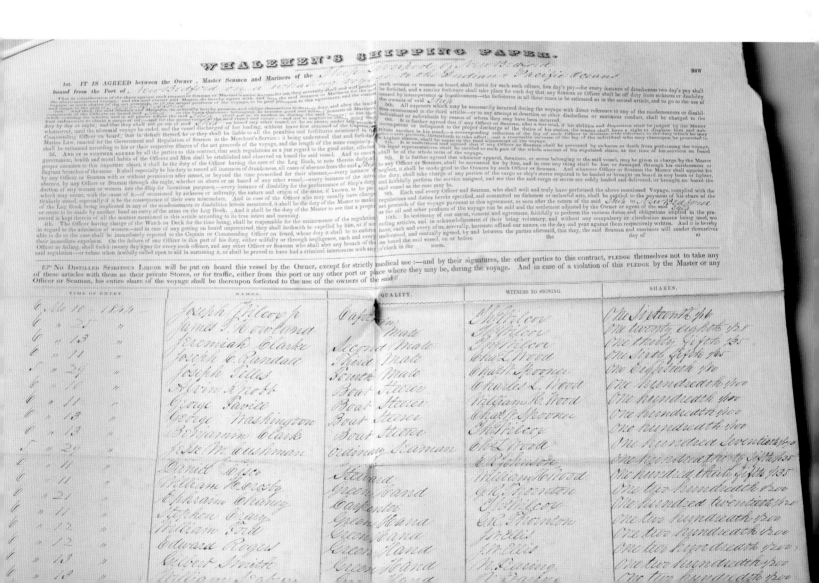

Much of what we know of whaling comes from reading official logbooks, journals, account books (financial transactions) and "outfitting books." A journal might have been kept by anyone who wished to record the day-to-day life aboard the whaler.

Entry:

Sunday 22nd good weather. At 8 oclock, this Evening Justus Root, breathed his last. every assistance was rendered in Our power which proved useless

The entry for the following day mentions fine weather, the lowering of boats, the taking of whales, cutting them in, and stowing some oil. After the hunting, the whaleboats took Justus Root's remains to a nearby shore for burial.

CANVAS BAG

Martha's Vineyard Museum

A skilled hand stitched this bag. The light sailcloth is fitted with brass grommets at the mouth. The generous, light line seems to form a shoulder strap. It suggests that it may have been used for carrying long items aloft (possibly tools or a telescope) while leaving both hands free for climbing.

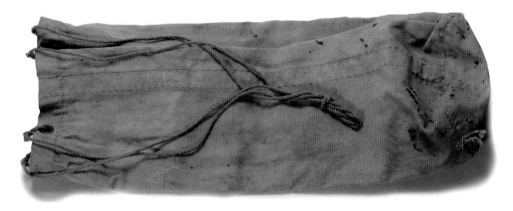

MONUMENT TO LOST WHALEMAN—JOHN E. HOWELL

Two Views
Sag Harbor Cemetery

John E. Howell,
Born March 2, 1813
Died July 22, 1840
While Engaged in the Whale Fishery
In the Pacific Ocean
In Command of the Ship FRANCE
He lost his life
In an encounter with a Sperm Whale
In the 28th year of His Age

Erected by
Nathan P., Gilbert and Augustus
In Remembrance of their brother
1856

The monument was erected sixteen years after the loss of Captain Howell. It was not uncommon for the captain of the ship to act as officer on one of the whaleboats. This monument also recognizes several other Sag Harbor whalers who were lost at sea.

The imagery of the broken mast is symbolic of the loss felt by the family. Below the foot of the mast—carved in stone—are the tools of the trade, the double flued harpoon and the lance.

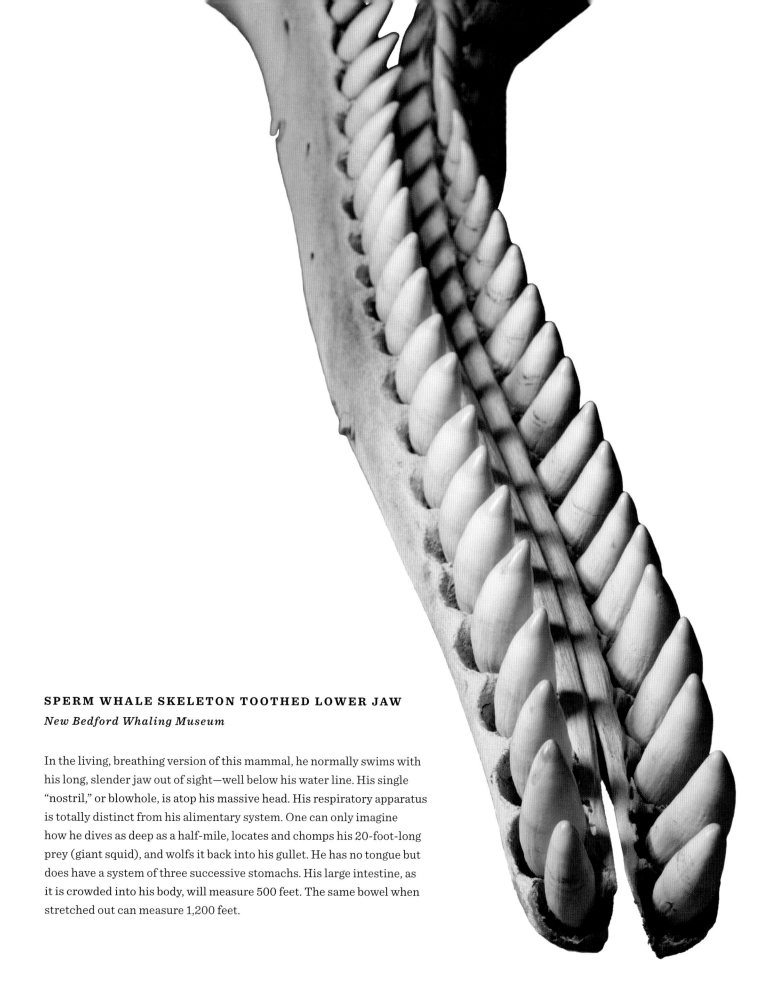

SPERM WHALE SKELETON TOOTHED LOWER JAW
New Bedford Whaling Museum

In the living, breathing version of this mammal, he normally swims with his long, slender jaw out of sight—well below his water line. His single "nostril," or blowhole, is atop his massive head. His respiratory apparatus is totally distinct from his alimentary system. One can only imagine how he dives as deep as a half-mile, locates and chomps his 20-foot-long prey (giant squid), and wolfs it back into his gullet. He has no tongue but does have a system of three successive stomachs. His large intestine, as it is crowded into his body, will measure 500 feet. The same bowel when stretched out can measure 1,200 feet.

Chapter Five

WHALES

Predators' eyes usually face forward. Man's eyes face forward. The whale's eyes do not. The position of a whale's eyes at the sides of his massive head leaves him vulnerable to attack from carefully observed "blind spots." When on the surface of the water, the whale relies on his extremely acute sense of hearing to alert him to activity anywhere near his gigantic body. The hunter, miniscule in comparison, used his intelligence, human arrogance, craftiness, stealth and tools to mount his assault. Slowly, by trial and error, he learned the whale's habits, quirks and behavioral characteristics in order to better his chance of success in stalking the behemoth.

The whale's defensive reactions are several. He can "sound" by lifting his giant tail (flukes) into the air, lowering his head into the water and making a deep, determined dive. Alternately, he can simply submerge with little effort other than closing his breathing hole. If he chooses to merely flee over the water's surface, he is capable of both speed and stamina. Particularly frustrating to his sailorman pursuer is his inbred tendency to swim "to windward."

The *right whale* has incredible dexterity with his tail. He can sweep it laterally along the water surface, violently dashing anything in its path. Lashing out "from eye to eye," as the whalemen would say. The mighty *sperm whale* had somewhat less flexibility in his defensive tail but could "fight with both ends." His slender, toothed lower jaw could snap sideways at a 30-foot wooden whaleboat and crunch it like a dried cracker.

This air-breathing, warm-blooded mammal is able to spend long periods below, but eventually he must rise to the surface. After thirty minutes or more in the depths, his rise is announced by his enormous exhalation of breath followed by successive greedy drafts of air. Quickly, however, his respiration becomes quite even.

The hunter learned the limits of the whale's time below. He noted the duration of each "sounding" and calculated the time on the surface that was required for the whale to fully "catch his breath" before sounding again. The ship's lookout men would report the behavior of distant pods of whales and note whether they were "feeding," "making a passage," "sleeping," "gallied" (frightened) or, sometimes, merely "playing." An experienced eye could note the approximate number in the pod, the species (from its distinctive spout shape), the direction of travel, distance from the ship, even the presence of bulls, cows and calves. Changes in behavior were called out to the officers below (often the officers were aloft as well!):"There she sounds"; "There she breaches"; "There she whitewaters." These were much more than casual observations. They informed the strategy and the tactics of the hunt. In time, every observation and each bit of knowledge gained about whale activity was recorded. Over the decades this lore was shared among the hunters, often "father to son" as they worked to gain advantage.

The whale is most in his element when he swims in the deep water far from land. Man, primarily a creature of the land, used whatever he knew of the elements, the winds, the sands, the shoals and the tides in the battle for the whale's life.

Man's original contact with whales would have been observing live ones that approached the inlets and shores. He would have been both mesmerized and appalled at the sight of a "drift whale," a dead whale rotting in the shallows. He would have both feared and envied the might it had when it swam the deep waters. Hunting, originally, may have been to prove that man was equal to the whale's immense power. Besides gratifying the hunter's ego, the prize from a successful kill would have been food, oily fat that readily burned, and useful body parts.

The kingdom of the whale genus is vast and varied. There are a great number of toothless *baleen whales*; of these, the right whale and the humpback whale were pursued. The prizes were their blubber and the flat plates that grew in their mouths with which they filtered their tiny food source, krill, from the seawater. This "baleen" was generally (and incorrectly) known as "whalebone." The third and mightiest species that was hunted was the sperm whale. It did not strain its food. It dove to great depths for giant squid, its preferred food. The giant mouth had a ferocious lower jaw with two rows of sharp ivory teeth (no upper teeth). The oil that was extracted from its fat and an enormous liquid reservoir in its head was of superb quality. The sperm whale was the ultimate prize.

Excerpt from Logbook for Grace *by Robert Cushman Murphy*
(1887–1973)

———◆———

ON THE SWIM MECHANICS
OF THE SPERM WHALE

October 1, 1912
Lat. 07° 55′ N., long. 24° W.

At nine o'clock this morning a big sperm whale was sighted, going quickly to windward and blowing out conspicuous and regular spouts. While three boats were being lowered, he crossed our bow at close range and I had a superb view of him from halfway up the rigging. His progression was marked by a gentle rocking or pitching, the blunt junk and the hump on the after-back alternately rising and falling. The flukes did not break the surface at any stage of their stroke. The appearance of ease, smoothness, and speed was exceedingly impressive.

The first sign of the forward end on the upswing was usually the spout, which burst forth a split second before the tip of the snout was exposed. The spout was slanted in the direction of the whale's course, and it fountained out for at least two seconds, perhaps longer. Mainly condensed vapor, it included also a basal spray of water due to the fact that violent expulsion of the breath began before the spiracle had quite reached the open air. This is contrary to what the books describe to us.

When the snout was at its high point, possibly eighteen inches above the water, I could see the mound made by the dilated lips of the single nostril as air was sucked back into the lungs. Then the whole head rocked slowly down, the long back rose and leveled, and the gleaming but curiously crinkled and rubbery skin showed clearly. Finally, the angular hump pitched into view, for a moment exposing also several of the lesser knobs and notches that lie along the crest of the back between hump and flukes. When the hump was highest, the submerged junk was lowest, and vice versa. . . .

[A] quatrain from Moby Dick came to mind . . .

> *Oh the rare old whale, mid storm and gale*
> *In his ocean home will be*
> *A giant in might, where might is right*
> *And King of the boundless sea.*

EAR BONE OF SPERM WHALE

Sag Harbor Whaling Museum

Some whaleman had a strong opinion that the whale had no ear. Evolution must have favored a sleek skin that would glide through the water because the actual external ear orifice is described as a slight indentation, just aft of the eye, as if made by a pencil eraser. Anatomical studies show that, indeed, the ears and their neural connections to the brain provide the sperm whale with the equipment needed for an acute sense of hearing.

The bone, here shown at life-size, is the tympanic bulla, which functions as an eardrum.

SPERM WHALE LOWER JAW SECTION

Falmouth Museum

These six teeth are still embedded in what originally could be called the animal's "gums"; in its current state, that tissue has hardened like bone. We are able to see the amount of each tooth that projects above the gum line. The larger teeth on the left would be toward the front of the whale's mouth. The arc shape of each tooth points back toward his mouth.

The animal generally has teeth only in the lower jaw. Where each tooth meets the upper part of the jaw there is a bit of a "socket" that matches the tooth shape. The whale does not truly masticate or chew his food, but there is some indication that he uses muscles in the soft upper jaw to oppose the teeth and shred food (such as the giant squid) before gulping it down. It's clear that the long lower jaw with up to fifty-two teeth is a fearsome weapon against whalers, or in battles with rivals of its own species. It is also a formidable defensive tool against any other marine enemy that would dare a confrontation.

TWO LOWER JAWS OF SPERM WHALES
Nantucket Whaling Museum

The lower jaw of a juvenile or baby sperm whale still has the teeth, gums and bone. A specimen from a larger animal that has teeth and gums, but no bone, straddles it. A mass "extraction" of the larger teeth as we see here was common. The entire lower jaw was hoisted on board and put aside until after the blubber had been recovered and its oil stowed away. The panbone itself was fastened to rings bolted into the deck, and the winch, or windlass, was used to pull up the entire row such as we see here. As "scrimshanding" grew in popularity, a whaler might be "awarded" a tooth or given even a piece of the panbone to decorate. This would provide endless hours of recreation.

The tooth count on the smaller example would seem to be twenty-six to a side for a total of fifty-two. A few on the right side seem to be broken away or otherwise missing, which frustrates an accurate count. The "fifty-two" total is frequently observed on museum specimens, but a range of forty to fifty-two teeth is often cited.

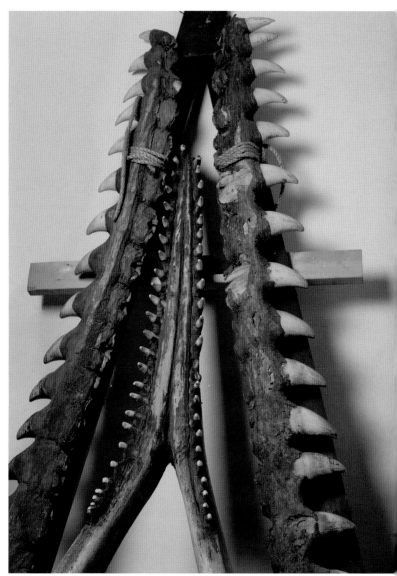

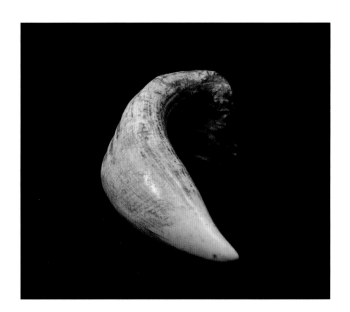

LARGE DEFORMED SPERM WHALE TOOTH
Cold Spring Harbor Whaling Museum

The size of this tooth would indicate that the whale was a successful enough food hunter to grow to maturity.

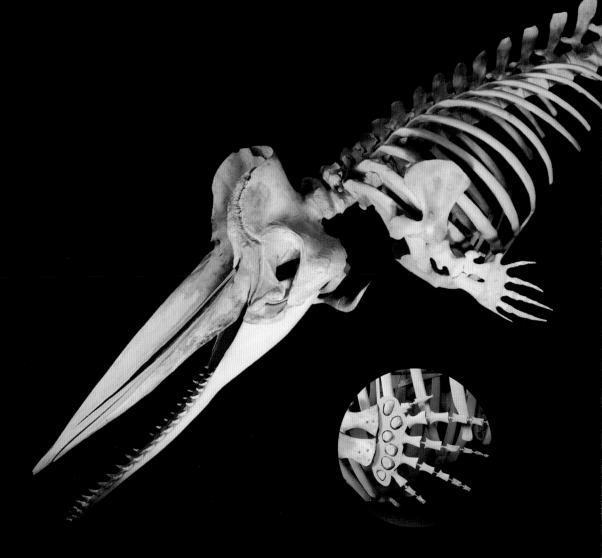

COMPLETE SPERM WHALE SKELETON

Great Hall

Nantucket Whaling Museum

DETAIL—FLIPPER BONES

New Bedford Whaling Museum

The beaked upper and lower jaws are bird-like. Their shape also resembles that of the bottlenose dolphin, a relative. The image of a living, breathing sperm whale is not immediately obvious when we look at this 50-foot skeleton. In life, the tissue that makes up its enormous head and the cartilage that shapes the 16-foot flukes give the mammal its signature look. The entire massive "forehead" (comedians might call it a "fivehead") is soft tissue with no bones. This "negative space" that we must visualize as we look at just the bones contains the "spermaceti organ," which makes up over 25 percent of the sperm whale's anatomy. Scientists speak of the foremost part of the head as the bulbous "nose." Whalers knew that just below the surface of the whale's head was a reservoir (the "case") that held an enormous supply (600 gallons was typical) of a pure semiliquid: spermaceti oil. Biologists or chemists would say that it is more correctly described as a wax. Whalers also knew that additional ultravaluable product was to be found in the head, adjacent to the reservoir of spermaceti. They carefully isolated the parts that they called the "whitehorse" and the "junk." Unlike the spermaceti, which could be stored with little or no processing, the supplies air to the lungs. The "right nasal passage" supplies an air-filled cushion as well as a "distal air sac through a valve-like clapper system, the museau du singe ('monkey muzzle')." When submerged, the sperm whale squeezes air past these "phonic lips" and creates a constant "chatter" of clicks and related sounds. This "voice" is certainly used to communicate but is also believed to be used for echolocation. It can be used in relation to the whale's immediate surroundings or over great distances. It's believed that the spermaceti organ and the junk with "a series of acoustic lenses" can "broadcast" sounds and then use the same equipment, as well as the lower jaw and skeletal bones, to "receive" return echoes. These data are reported to the enormous brain, which is believed to convert them into useful images for the whale. "The spermaceti organ extends the sperm whale's sensory environment far out into the ocean."

Scientists who have studied the sperm whale note that its olfactory sense is virtually nonexistent—if it has any sense of smell at all, it is likely very small. The "nose," as previously noted, has evolved into "the greatest sonar system in the animal kingdom." Likewise, the sense of taste does not seem to be very highly developed. The animal's sense of hearing when on the surface was known by whalers to be extremely acute. His eyesight, which is useful mainly at the surface or at shallow depths, is considered quite good. Whalers compared the size of his eyeball to that of an ox.

The sperm whale is remarkable in that it is a mammal that evolved from ancestors that lived on the land. It still exhibits a vestigial pelvic girdle that would indicate the location of hind legs. In the skeleton (*above*) an iron rod holds this bone in its approximate position—beneath the tail vertebrae. The bones of his flipper bear a startling resemblance to those in the human hand. The sperm whale has been known to hold its breath for up to ninety minutes, and dives deeper than a mile have been verified. He has a remarkable circulatory system and temperature regulator. Ironically, as he dives into the frigid depths, his need is to keep cool rather than to stay warm. The blubber that surrounds his enormous muscle mass acts to insulate and hold in the heat generated by the exertion of diving and swimming.

SMALL BALEEN SAMPLE
Wellfleet Historical Society

Clifford W. Ashley (1881–1947) was a New Bedford whaleman who went on to become a noted painter of whaling life, as well as an author. His 1926 book *The Yankee Whaler* stands as a great document of the whaling trade.

Ashley quotes an old whaling friend, a Mr. Smith, who had a remarkably simple view of whale classification:

"There are only two kinds of whale"—
"One of 'em is the Sperm Whale; the rest of 'em is the other."

Nantucket and New Bedford men loved to hunt the sperm whale. They respected it as a wily and intrepid foe. When the battle was won, they stowed down oil that would put "top dollar" in their pocket.

The sperm whale, alone of the great whales that were hunted, has a *toothed* lower jaw. It has no baleen. It dives deep in the ocean for its food. Toothed whales are of the suborder Odontoceti (whales with teeth).

Baleen whales skim through the water and take in great quantities of it in search of small particles of food like tiny crustaceans known as krill, plus plankton and small fish. Very long "plates" of what was called "whalebone" were attached to the roof of the whale's mouth. The trailing edge of each plate had fibrous wisps such as we see below. Thousands of the plates acted in concert to filter out the food as the whale expelled the water. A thick fringe of fiber can still be visible when the whale's mouth is shut. This gives rise to the name for the suborder of baleen whales: Mysticeti—whales with mustaches.

There was no "romance" associated with the harvest of baleen, or whalebone. Thousands of pounds could be hacked from the mouth of a single animal. The sharpened "bone spade" was the tool that was used. Once brought on deck, the plates, sometimes over 10 feet long, would have to be scrubbed and dried before being bound into loose bundles to permit the circulation of air. The substance was an ideal "medium" for the culture of bacteria. Just the humidity of the hold where the "bone" was stored could give rise to mold and mildew. This, of course, would greatly lower its price at the marketplace. It was a dreaded chore to bring the entire contaminated cargo back up on deck so that it could be scrubbed, washed, dried and bundled, once again. Also, the oil that was tried out from the baleen whales—the right, the humpback, the gray, the bowhead and others—was valued at about half of that of the sperm whale.

SPERM WHALE TOOTH, TWO VIEWS

Nantucket Whaling Museum

"Captured Off Western Coast of Australia by Bark *Kathleen*." The whale that owned the tooth is presumably what was captured, not the graceful damsel that is shown on the reverse side.

AMBERGRIS SAMPLE
Martha's Vineyard Museum

Perfume is known to be concocted from scores (sometimes *hundreds*) of fragrant essences, extracts and other aromatic compounds. Ambergris, an "oxidized fatty compound," has long been used in perfumery to "fix" and "bind" the various substances and allow them to work together. It is equally useful (and valuable) whether it is found in a rubbery and gelatinous state, or as we see here, hardened like a lump of coal.

Whalers were especially watchful for the presence of ambergris when they had taken an obviously sick or emaciated sperm whale. The substance is thought to be secreted along ulcerated or unhealthy tissue in the whale's stomach or bowel. Sharp "beaks" of cuttlefish or giant squid (favorite foods) are often found commingled with lumps of ambergris.

"SECRET" AMBERGRIS HANDBILL OFFERS $50 IN GOLD TO FINDERS
Martha's Vineyard Museum

This unsigned, printed treatise was obviously created by a major shipowner or whaling-company figure. It has fill-in-the-blanks capacity, and here is addressed to Captain Chas. L. Downs of the whaling bark *Minnesota*.

It is a clarion call to search for ambergris with each sperm whale taken. It explains exactly what is to be looked for—and the value of the substance at market. (It should be remembered that all hands were working for a share in the profits from the voyage.) It seems that the author would have the captains collect virtually *all* feces from each whale's 500-foot intestine in the belief that it would be transformed into ambergris and could be sold for a spectacular price.

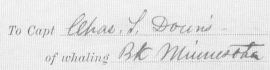

To Capt *Chas. L. Downs*
of whaling *Bk Minnesota*

In regard to Ambergris, I hope you keep a sharp look out at the time of killing every sperm whale, as well as when cutting him in. Our bark Perry took 44 lbs. from one sperm whale; Capt. Nickerson sent it home and it was sold for $175 per lb., and netted nearly $7,740. The white and black are just as good, or nearly so, as the gray or yellow. Buyers of it however, always try to depreciate the white and black, and call it inferior, but others more honest, say it is just as good. The lot from bark Perry all brought about one price, the white, black and yellow, and as we have since learned, it is all nearly equal in value. In looking for it, some only take from the intestines the hard portions of it, discarding the soft, white and black, and seemingly refuse portions. This is a great error, as any portions thus rejected are worth from $100 to $200 per lb., and the very best may be found in that condition. In London, I learn the best quality will bring from $200 to $320 per lb. It is said by those who have looked into the subject, that the very dung of the sperm whale, before it becomes hardened into the hard substances called Ambergris, is just as much Ambergris as the hardened lumps. Therefore you will please collect all substances from the sperm whale's intestines and barrel them up with care, for shipment home. And when the known article of Ambergris is found, save every ounce of refuse, soft waste stuff, there is in the intestine, whether it is white, black, gray or yellow, or any other color.

It is said that the sperm whale, when struck and lanced, and spouting blood, that, at this time will involuntarily discharge the Ambergris in his bowels, and therefore his discharges should be watched until he is safely along-side the ship; even then careful examinations should be made, less the Ambergris is discharged unobserved while cutting in the whale. Such was the opinion of Capt. Geo. W. Nickerson, master of bark Perry, who had been a party to the discovery of Ambergris on three different voyages. He says in his opinion much Ambergris is lost in both of these ways, not being noticed in the excitement that accompanies this class of work, first in killing the whale and towing to the ship, and also in cutting in. He believes it is often overlooked and not observed at such times. Capt. Edward Hicks, late master of the bark Sea Queen, and Andrew Hicks, who has taken more or less Ambergris on every voyage, told me that he has taken 270 lbs. Ambergris from one small sperm whale that made only 12 bbls. of oil. That on that voyage they took altogether 370 lbs. He also says that in searching for it, he once had a man to run his foot into the intestine the whole length of the man's body, and in that way had taken out considerable lumps of it. It is believed that it will pay to cut open the whale as far as possible and search for it in the intestine that leads out of the body. In fact it is believed by some experts, and by some medical men, that any dung, whether in a liquid state, or in harder substance, on being dried will become Ambergris.

You are authorized to offer a bounty of $50 in gold, to any of the officers or crew of *Bk Minnesota* who shall first discover any Ambergris in any considerable quantity, either floating on the water while killing a whale, or towing a whale, or in cutting in a whale, or otherwise. The above bounty will be paid on the collection of 10 lbs. and upwards of Ambergris, from any of the above named chances. On the collection of 50 lbs. and upwards, $100 in gold will be paid, and you are hereby authorized to pay the same.

This document belongs to *Bk Minnesota* and you are directed to keep it on board among the accounts of the vessel.

I have obtained this information about Ambergris at great care, and some expense. I have had it printed for my own use, and the use of our vessels. I do not show it to other ship-masters, as the information contained is my own. Besides, if it should be found in large quantities, by many ships, it would materially lessen the price. Therefore this paper must be kept a secret; but you can tell your officers and crew the substance of it, but act fully and sharply upon it yourself. I have got it up for ship-masters only, who are or may be in my employ. If you shall succeed in finding any large quantity of Ambergris, or of the refuse material described, please not report it to the world, and be careful that it shall not be told any parties who may publish it; but keep all information as to quantity, a secret, as the market price is very sensitive, and will be materially changed on the discovery of much of it.

CASE BAILER
Martha's Vineyard Museum

A look at a sperm whale's skeleton will show that nearly one-third of his or her length is "head." The bulbous sac or membrane that held the huge quantity of spermaceti was known as the case. The afterpart of the carcass was frequently severed so that the two parts could be worked separately.

If conditions of vessel size, whale size and weather were all favorable, the preferred method of extracting the spermaceti could be employed.

The severed head would be winched into position alongside the cutting stage with its snout pointing toward the sky. A slit was opened at the topmost part of the case. The sturdy tapered bucket shown here would be dangled over the case with ropes hanging from a sturdy (but flexible) "whip" of wood.

Like "drawing water from a well," the bailer would make *hundreds* of dips—deeper and deeper—into the case (possibly as deep as 20 feet) to save every drop of the spermaceti. After the bailing was completed, the case, now a giant, slippery bladder, would be carefully extracted from the head and brought aboard to be worked further.

CARVED WOODEN WHALE-TRADE SIGN
Just Folk Antiques
SANTA BARBARA, CALIFORNIA

This whale hung for years above a merchant's doorway in New Bedford. Its anatomical inaccuracies are readily overlooked in favor of its whimsy and "folk art" charm. The carver positioned a natural knot in the wood to be the eye. The shape of the jaw, the grooves carved into the fin and the tail flukes as well as the upper row of teeth are fanciful creations. The longitudinal cracks, or "checking" are to be expected from a solid piece of wood left exposed to the elements hanging from the chunky, forged chain and hooks.

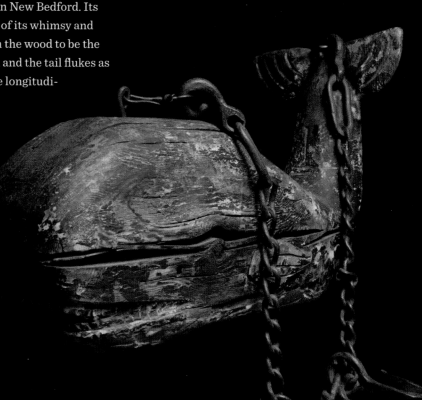

**DOUBLE-FLUED HARPOON
DRAMATICALLY TWISTED
FROM THE ACTION OF A WHALE**
Nantucket Whaling Museum

This iron records the whale's incredible struggle to be free. We don't know the final outcome, but one man, the blacksmith, ably made his contribution.

The flues would have been treated in such a way that the metal could be honed to a fine sharpness. The shank would have been given a different temper so that it could bend (as we see) and hold fast without breaking. One test that was sometimes used in evaluating a smith's skill would be to attempt to wrap the wrought iron of the shank around a bar with just a 1-inch diameter.

Chapter Six

WHALECRAFT AND THE TOOLS OF WHALING

T he sooty open-air workshop along the Massachusetts coast in the nineteenth century may have *looked* like the village smithy, but quite often the trade sign would read WHALECRAFT. The industry here was not shoeing horses, repairing plows and buggy springs, but fashioning weapons for the whale hunt.

The shipowners preparing for a long cruise into distant waters knew from experience what was required. The hand-darted harpoon was the primary tool. The blacksmith knew that every inch of its length was vital. The razor-sharp leading edge of the "iron" was expected to cause an entrance wound into possibly 2 feet of surprisingly dense, tough, fibrous blubber—and continue into the ani-

mal's flesh. Once so embedded, it was expected to stay "fast" and resist "drawing out" through the same wound. The hemp or manila "whale line" was securely hitched onto the iron at the "socket"— the tapered cup or ferrule that received the stout wooden handle. The shank of the iron, a rod about 3 feet long, connected the barbed tip and this socket. The shank was fashioned of a ductile but tough wrought iron that would allow the embedded iron to safely bend and lie back longitudinally against the fleeing whale's body. The expectation was that the iron and the whale line would handle a strain of up to 6,000 pounds. The wooden handle was designed to fall away after the whale had been "struck."

The second required instrument was also a type of spear. It was a surgically sharpened "lance" on a very long iron rod. It was used to deliver the *coup de grâce* to the exhausted whale. The whaleboat would maneuver itself directly alongside of the surfaced beast, just aft of its side fin. The officer would find the gap between ribs and plunge the weapon deep into the whale's innards in search of its "life." This is a general and imprecise area of the lungs and blood vessels where it was known that the whale could be killed. The whale's actual heart was considered to be too deeply situated in the body to be a target. The whaleboat would then withdraw to a safe distance as the mortally wounded animal went through his death agony, known as his flurry.

The term "whalecraft" refers to those instruments used in the taking and then the cutting in (butchering) of whales. These tools, primarily fashioned of forged iron, included harpoons, lances, cutting spades, mincing knives, boarding knives and blubber hooks. The category is often expanded to include other devices, such as cast-iron trypots and kettles plus copper and tin items like strainers, skimmers, funnels and other tools used in rendering the blubber into oil.

The catalogue of tools used in whaling actually stretches back for millennia. Man fashioned ingenious devices from the toolmaking material that he knew best: stone, bone, wood, fiber, sinew, antler and, eventually, metal. Innovations at the forge and foundry allowed the smith to create tools (weapons, really) that emboldened the whaler in his hunt.

As America began to grow, the phenomenon of the industrial revolution transformed certain activities, which had formerly been "folkcraft" into the "stuff of engineers." Inventions designed to improve the whaling industry abounded. The thrifty Yankee whalemen did not jump at each and every innovation fresh from the Patent Office, but they were quick to adopt any tool that increased their success at fastening to and "saving" (also known as killing) whales.

SINGLE-FLUE AND
DOUBLE-FLUE IRONS
Wellfleet Historical Society

Wellfleet is a protected Massachusetts harbor
just below Provincetown at the very tip of Cape
Cod. The origin of the town name is uncertain,
but one theory is that it's a corruption of "whale
fleet." The stranding of whales on the shallows
of Cape Cod Bay has been happening for as long
as history has been recorded. Pilot whales, also
known as blackfish, get trapped on the receding
tides on almost a yearly basis. Native Americans
and early settlers regarded the arrival of the small,
toothed whales as a bonanza. They harvested the
meat and processed the fine-quality oil. Today
rescue teams attempt to coax the whales back into
deeper water.

The crooked shanks of these old irons show
that they've seen some action.

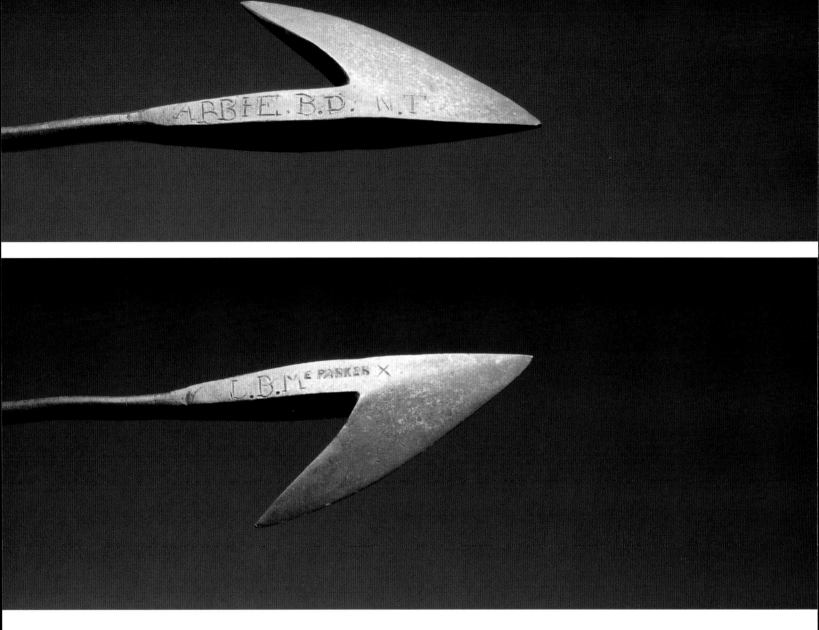

SINGLE-FLUE IRON, TWO VIEWS
Nantucket Whaling Museum

Here it's probably best to call this a variation in design rather than an improvement. In theory, the single sharpened leading edge creates an entry wound that is half the width of a double flue. Then, as the animal attempts his escape, the "fast" iron pulls back at an angle and "sets" itself. Conversely, one could argue that it only had half the holding power of a double flue. It must have been a matter of preference because the two weapons were in wide use for hundreds of years. The maker's mark has been stamped "E. Parker." A small x has been added after that.

SINGLE-FLUE IRON MARKED "S.N.P.T."
Nantucket Whaling Museum

A little sleuthing can turn up a surprising bit of information from just the four letters chiseled into this single flue iron. In this case it represents the Ship *Nathan P. Talmadge*. Knowing that, we can find out that she sailed from Poughkeepsie, New York, and also the dates that she set out on and returned from her several cruises.

If crews from competing ships were pursuing the same pod of whales, it became an important point of law to have your equipment so marked. It was also common for each boat crew to mark their respective gear.

DAMAGED DOUBLE-FLUED HARPOON HEAD
Nantucket Whaling Museum

The break here is likely due to metal fatigue. The location of the break is right at the point where the smith makes a "forged weld." He heats both the head and the shank to the exact required temperature and pounds them together. Sometimes pure white sand or some other "flux," such as borax, is mounded up around the two parts to keep impurities out and to allow the molecules to bond into a single piece. Cooling slowly would not be desirable for this tool, so it would be immediately "quenched" in a trough of (possibly) rainwater to bring the temperature down quickly and impart a consistent crystalline structure to the metal. An apprentice or unskilled blacksmith might not realize that there is a right and a wrong way to quench. The master smith will send it sizzling into the water, moving it in a swirling pattern so that cooler water is always drawing heat out of the weld. Holding the welded piece lazily in one static position can impart a fault in the iron, which can cause it to fail exactly as we see here.

The blubber harvested from a successful kill often had whalecraft (such as we see here) embedded from much earlier battles from which the whale ultimately escaped.

DISTRESSED TWO-FLUED IRON WITH BENT SHAFT

Nantucket Whaling Museum

Corrosion has taken place long after the tool's useful life. It reveals the sinewy nature of the wrought iron. The blacksmith achieves the strength and other properties he desires through folding and laminating the cherry-red iron through successive "heats" and hammer blows at his anvil. The bend in the shank was possibly the result of an encounter with a whale.

Smiths often forged a thin section in the shank at about the spot where the jog appears in this iron. It encourages the iron to bend and lie back along the fleeing animal's hide and thus increase the holding power. Such a planned bend also countered the tendency for the iron to withdraw through the entry wound.

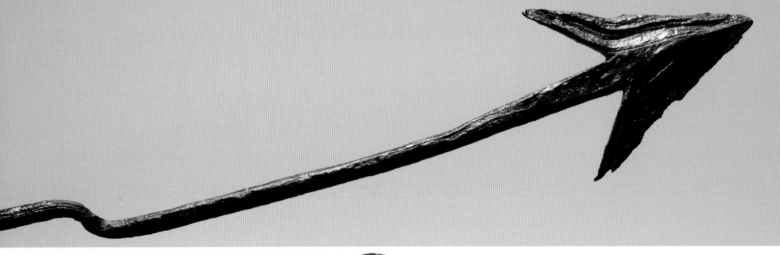

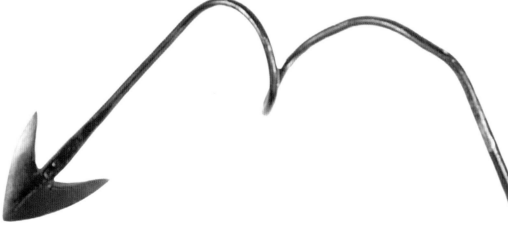

TWISTED DOUBLE-FLUED HARPOON

Nantucket Whaling Museum

It's probable that the straight section from the tip of the harpoon to the first bend shows the depth of the blubber (and possibly flesh) that has resisted all attempts to pull loose.

Even with a routine kill—where the iron gets fast to the whale, the whale runs ahead and is ultimately taken—the harpoon will be recovered but now be in the shape of an L or the numeral 7.

BENT DOUBLE-FLUED HARPOON
Martha's Vineyard Museum

This bent harpoon is yet another example of the battle between man and whale. We don't know if it stands as a trophy for a whale that was taken, or as an eloquent alibi for one that got away.

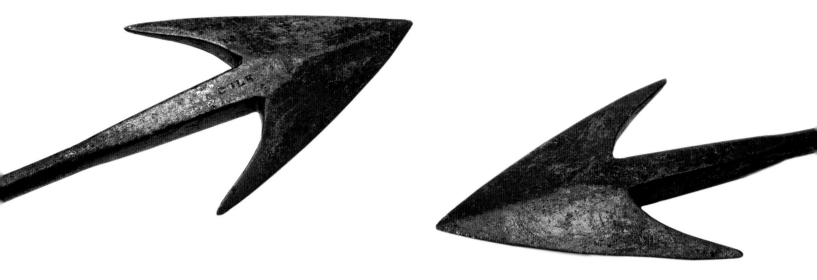

TWO-FLUED IRON STAMPED WITH BLACKSMITH'S IDENTIFICATION: "COLE"
Cold Spring Harbor Whaling Museum

Luther Cole and his son Edward R. Cole were well-known smiths in the latter part of the nineteenth century in New Bedford and across the Acushnet River in Fairhaven.

    Two views of the same iron here show a very smooth transition (forged weld) where the head joins the shank; this section is called the boss.

IMPROVED TOGGLE HARPOON SHOWING SOCKET SERVED WITH MARLINE
Cold Spring Harbor Whaling Museum

The socket is the critical point of attachment between the metal harpoon itself and the hemp or manila whale line being "paid out" from the whaleboat. Any slippage or a break here allows the whale to escape. The "serving" of the socket with marline works as a "chafing gear" to keep the fibers of the whale line from being worn away.

HARPOON WITH STOP WITHERS
Nantucket Whaling Museum

This iron is stamped with the maker's mark, "F.Smith." The style was popular with English whaling. The little reverse barbs called "stop withers" were thought to help prevent the iron from withdrawing as the whale went through its motions. The head is made from cast steel. The whole tool is considerably heavier than a typical Yankee harpoon.

The English whalers pursued the immense animal known variously as the Greenland right, Bowhead or Arctic right whale. Whale species living in colder waters tended to have a thicker blubber coat. Thus, the oil was more plentiful than that from a similar-size sperm whale but of lesser quality and lesser value.

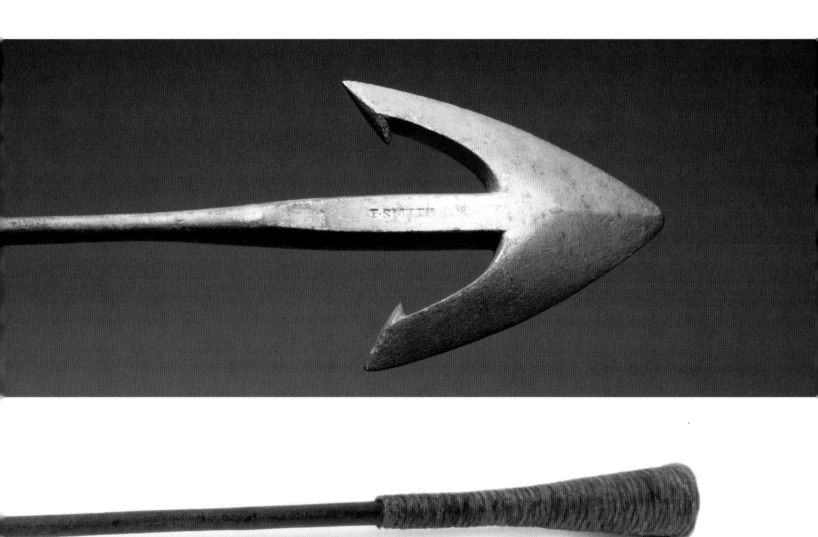

DOUBLE-FLUE IRON MARKED "ALABAMA," TWO VIEWS
Nantucket Whaling Museum

"Alabama" is marked on one side. The opposite side is marked with "XX" and the outline of the letter *F*. A "register" of visits to the port of Ebon in the Marshall Islands around 1862 records the *Alabama* as a Nantucket vessel under the command of Captain Alfred M. Coffin. Further entries show her in a return visit a year or two later.

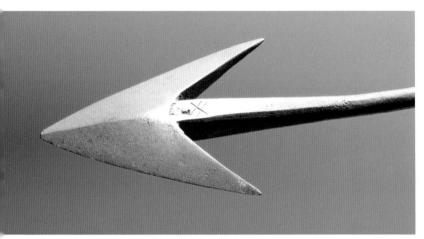
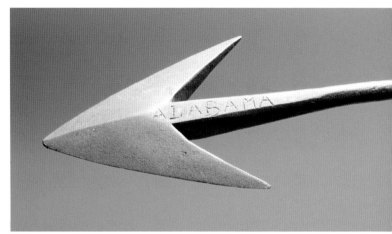

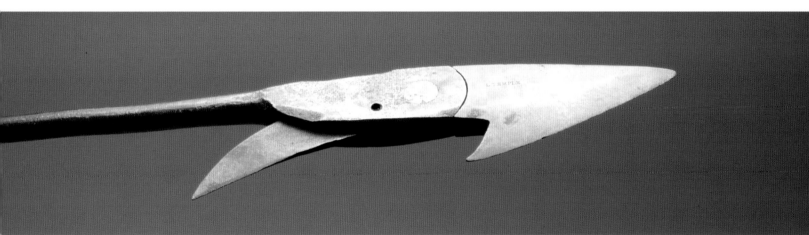

TEMPLE IRON WITH "TOGGLE HEAD"
Nantucket Whaling Museum

This revolutionary toggle-head iron is stamped with the most celebrated name in whalecraft design: L. Temple. Lewis Temple was the New Bedford blacksmith who in about 1848 began to supply his whaling customers with this radical innovation. It gained the name Temple's gig or the Temple iron. Its success in saving whales (an ironic term) caused it to become the standard harpoon in the industry. Most irons until this time had no moving parts. It's shown above in its darting position.

TEMPLE IRON IN "OPEN" POSITION
Nantucket Whaling Museum

The ideal was to have the toggle stay aligned, like the spear it is. When this iron has penetrated deeply and begins to feel the strain of the attached line, the toggle head pivots and forms the T shape shown here.

To prevent this from happening before the dart has achieved maximum depth, there were two safety mechanisms that could be employed. First, a wrap or two of light cord (marline) could bind the movable head to the shank just aft of the pivot pin. It was tied against a sharpened edge that had a single purpose: to sever this cord when the first reverse strain was felt—allowing the toggle to switch to this T position and hold fast in the blubber. Second, a peg of wood—a matchstick would do the job—would be inserted when the small holes, visible here, aligned. Here the strain would shear the little peg and allow the head to move, as described. As the effectiveness of the Temple iron was proven, it spawned dozens of other attempts at innovation. Later the wooden peg alone was most frequently employed to hold the darting position.

One frequently reads that of every seven whales to which hunters actually "got fast" only about one was ultimately saved (killed and butchered). The Temple iron is said to have improved that score to *two* whales in seven saved. That was welcome news to the whalers.

Temple was an African-American. He was a successful harpooner before establishing himself as a business owner in New Bedford. His blacksmith shop was already prospering before his breakthrough innovation came in 1848. This was well before the Civil War would end slavery in the United States.

TEMPLE IRON (*LEFT*)
IMPROVED TEMPLE IRON MADE BY COLE (*RIGHT*)
Nantucket Whaling Museum

The improvement here probably has less to do with the tool's effectiveness in hunting and more to do with ease of manufacture and lower cost. The shank of the Temple iron required the forging of a clevis, or "cheek pieces." These had precisely punched holes, which, when aligned with the hole in the sharpened toggle head, received the pivot pin.

The improved iron (*right*) was assembled with a cast head. The shank now was simply a rod flattened at one end and punched with a hole. Note that the new head dispensed with the second sharpened edge as well. Both irons continued to use the small holes to hold the iron in darting position by insertion of a wooden peg. The lower item is stamped with the maker's name—Cole—the New Bedford whalecraft maker.

Temple himself incorporated the improvements in accordance with the wishes of his customers. His shop records indicate that he produced over 10,000 irons.

THREE DESIGNS, KILLING LANCES
Cold Spring Harbor Whaling Museum

The "endgame" in a whale hunt would involve the man in the bow who darted the harpoon (the boat-steerer) switching places with the mate (the boatheader) who had been in the stern manning the long steering oar and barking commands. The mate sauntered forward and was handed the long spear that had a single purpose—finding that part of the whale's innards known as its life—and ending the battle.

The design of this weapon combined a scalpel-sharp blade (we see three different types here), a long, thin rod of wrought iron (the shank), which was permanently affixed to a wooden pole. There was a short warp of rope attached, but the lance was not meant to be darted or to leave the mate's grip.

TWO KILLING LANCES
Nantucket Whaling Museum

Lances were typically 5 to 6 feet long from tip to socket. The wooden handle would bring the total length to about 12 feet. The upper weapon shown here was known as a "dollar lance"—not because of the price but because the size and shape of the tip matched that of a silver dollar.

The giant captured mammal wheezed with exhaustion on the surface. The men pulled at their oars or strained with their paddles to bring the whaleboat within a few feet of the great whale's fin and baseball-sized eye. The mate was positioned in the bow and was handed the long lance. He had only to find his mark between two ribs and drive the scalpel-sharp instrument deep into the beast's anatomy. He sought the whale's "life."

There are accounts of the mate plunging the metal blade and shank their full 6-foot length and then casually "churning" the protruding wooden stock, causing the sharpened head to find artery, vein and lung. That business done, the boat was quickly withdrawn to a safer distance to allow the whale his death flurry.

RAZOR-SHARP DOLLAR LANCE
Blacksmith's Reproduction
Pete Oliva, Blacksmith
S&P Harpoons, Sutton, Alaska

Items of whalecraft that survive in museums and other collections frequently share two traits—they are dull and rusty.

Alaska blacksmith Pete Oliva has forged a highly accurate replica of the "dollar lance." This example has been given an edge that is frighteningly sharp.

Herman Melville observed that every harpooneer carried a whetstone in his pocket.

Lances, when made ready for their deadly task, would also be greased. A deprecating comment on a poor or unlucky whaleship was "They haven't got enough oil on that ship to grease their lances."

THREE SHOES, OR SCABBARDS, FOR LANCES OR HARPOONS

Nantucket Whaling Museum

These wooden "keepers" are covered with a light canvas cloth and painted. The "SB" initials signify "starboard boat."

The edges of harpoons, cutting spades, lances and other working tools were kept surgically sharp. Great care was taken to prevent accidents both aboard ship and in the crowded, often chaotic, conditions in the working whaleboat. The two "live" irons darted at the whale remained a hazard to the men after a kill. The first could still be where it was first planted. It continued to be a hazard during the butchering until it was safely extracted and covered. The second iron might never have been fastened to the whale at all, but it was still attached to the snarl of line around the kill—an "accident waiting to happen."

BLACKSMITH MADE METAL SCRAPER

Wellfleet Historical Society

A busy whaleship saw a constant cycle of horrendous filth followed by a return to shipshape cleanliness. Every scrap of blubber was destined for the kettles to extract the oil. After the oil had been "tried out" it was allowed to cool and then stowed away in the hold below decks. Soot, cinders and ash from the roaring fires adhered to spars, sails, decks, clothing and the men. All hands were tasked to return the vessel to a spotless condition to assure the purity of the next oil that would be rendered.

This simple, flat piece of metal riveted to a four-foot handle would function as scraper, squeegee and dustpan.

BLACKSMITH-MADE GRAPNEL
Cold Spring Harbor Whaling Museum

"Grapnel" is a nautical term. A similar tool on land might be called a grapple or grappling hook. A sturdier version than we see here might be used as a light, temporary anchor.

A close look and a bit of imagination allow us to see how the smith fashioned this from a single piece of flat iron bar. One "heat" is probably all it took to taper one end and fashion the loop that we see at the top. With subsequent "heats" he split the bar into threes and then tapered each and formed them into the treble hook. The elegant reverse curl at each tip undoubtedly served some specific purpose. It gives each hook slightly less tendency to pierce whatever is being retrieved (which could be anything at all). A typical use would be to gather the great coils of whale line floating in the water after a pursuit. The whaleboat was usually equipped with a similar grapnel mounted on a pole for retrieving equipment that floated nearby.

BOARDING KNIFE AND SCABBARD

Cold Spring Harbor Whaling Museum

The first hole cut into the blubber as the whale floats along the side of the ship would be made by a cutting spade. The boarding knife had two special functions up on deck.

Tension would be gradually applied to the spiral "scarf" of blubber as the winch took it higher and higher onto a boom supported by the mainmast. When the blubber reached its highest point, the continuous blanket of thick blubber that had been wrested and ripped loose might measure 25 feet long by about 3 feet wide. The strain on the mainmast would cause the whole ship to lean toward the whale being worked. The boarding knife could then be used to pierce the blubber just above deck level and slice a hole about 6 inches in diameter for insertion of the second hook. When all was tensioned properly, warning would be given that they were about to "board" the first piece. The man wielding the knife like a samurai sword would stay clear as he made the cut. The tons of blubber would swing aboard violently. The ship would bob upright. The piece would end up just over the "blubber parlor"—a large room belowdecks where it could be temporarily stored (skin side down).

The tool shown here was forged into a single piece of iron, with the socket providing a grip for one hand. The metal socket is securely pinned to the wooden handle. The bit of fancy ropework called the Turk's head knot kept the worker's hand safely from the blade. The T crossbar at the very end would be useful in cutting the small hole for the blubber hook. When not in use, the fearsome blade was kept in its wooden scabbard and stowed in the mate's quarters.

MINCING KNIFE WITH WOODEN BLADE GUARD
Cold Spring Harbor Whaling Museum

The blanket pieces would be reduced in size to "horse pieces." Depending on the thickness of the blubber, they might be rectangles measuring 12 by 18 inches. They should be a size that can be managed with a blubber fork as they are added to the boiling trypots. Before boiling they were "minced" with the two-handled knife seen here.

Hand mincing was a two-man job. A cutting board called the "mincing horse" straddled a holding tub or container. One man used a gaff to advance the piece a bit at a time as the other brought this blade up and down guillotine-style. Each cut stopped just short of the skin side. The horse piece now had a much greater surface area, which helped extract the oil more quickly. The flaps of blubber now resembled pages of a book and were known as "bible pieces."

PORPOISE IRON WITH SWIVEL BARB
Cold Spring Harbor Whaling Museum

Certain porpoises would yield a small quantity of excellent oil. They were also hunted for food. This weapon has a hole drilled in the socket indicating that it was used as a spear. The barb would lie close to the shank when in darting position. With a short length of line attached, it would be possible to hunt from places on the ship.

The name "porpoise" was sometimes used in marketing products derived from the lovable white beluga. Inuits considered beluga meat (especially the skin) a delicacy. This whale could be killed by a gun fired from a boat as small as a canoe. It would then be harpooned to keep from sinking. It had a hide that could be beautifully tanned and sold as "porpoise leather."

SWIVEL BARB IRON WITH IRON STRAP, TWO VIEWS
Cold Spring Harbor Whaling Museum

The design of this iron incorporates a small dart-shaped head to allow easy penetration into the whale with a pair of barbs that protrude very slightly. The barbs swivel out for improved holding power as the animal strains to pull free.

Significant here is the short length of rope called the "iron strap." When the full harpoon with wood handle is made up, this strap is usually tied with light line along the length of the wood with the eye splice toward the butt end. In action after it has been darted, the wooden handle separates and the light line breaks, leaving just the parts shown here attached to the whale and the whale line. The importance of this short attachment rope cannot be overstated. The harpooner has fashioned an eye splice at each end. The end that attaches to the iron may have a slightly larger loop. This loop is given a couple of expert turns to create the classic "double hitch and splice" attachment to the served socket. Thomas G. Lytle in his encyclopedic book *Harpoons and Other Whalecraft* points out that this swivel barb design was sometimes called a "porpoise iron," as it was used in hunting that smaller animal. The construction would employ pivot pins that were much lighter-duty, not the robust dimension required for whaling.

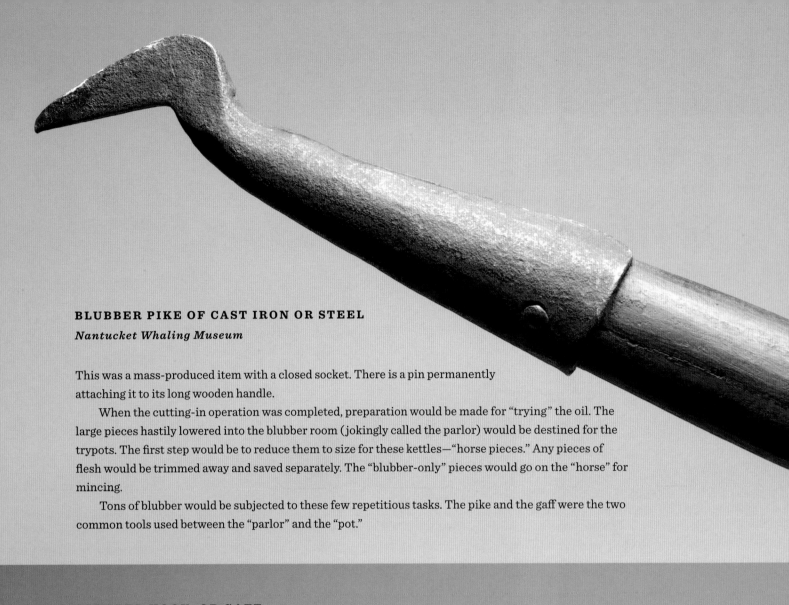

BLUBBER PIKE OF CAST IRON OR STEEL
Nantucket Whaling Museum

This was a mass-produced item with a closed socket. There is a pin permanently attaching it to its long wooden handle.

When the cutting-in operation was completed, preparation would be made for "trying" the oil. The large pieces hastily lowered into the blubber room (jokingly called the parlor) would be destined for the trypots. The first step would be to reduce them to size for these kettles—"horse pieces." Any pieces of flesh would be trimmed away and saved separately. The "blubber-only" pieces would go on the "horse" for mincing.

Tons of blubber would be subjected to these few repetitious tasks. The pike and the gaff were the two common tools used between the "parlor" and the "pot."

BLUBBER HOOK, OR GAFF
Nantucket Whaling Museum

This simple tool looks to have been quickly but expertly fashioned by a blacksmith. The wood still retains the sheen of animal fat.

COMBINATION TOOL, BLUBBER HOOK AND PIKE
Wellfleet Historical Society

This tool is stamped with the manufacturers' name—Cock Rhymes & Co. It sensibly combines two tools in one. It's about as long as a hockey stick. Generally, a whaleship would be outfitted with one tool for pushing blubber pieces—the pike—and another for pulling the pieces—the hook.

PIERCE DARTING GUN

Cold Spring Harbor Whaling Museum

This weapon marks a dramatic escalation in the assault on whales. A single powder charge (similar to a shotgun) sends two projectiles into the whale. The bomb lance is the cylindrical projectile with the sharp point. It is designed to explode after penetrating the whale, killing it almost instantly. The improved iron has been modified with a forged loop to which the whale line would be attached.

As weapons such as this came into use, the advantage shifted mightily to the whaler. The holocaust had begun and many whale species would be hunted to near-extinction.

BOMB LANCE
Nantucket Whaling Museum

For decades, firearms that shot a projectile (such as we see below) into the whale's innards were carried on the hunt even though "harpooning first—lancing later" continued to be the chosen method. Exploding projectiles were frequently judged too expensive or too unreliable (the powder easily got wet). When they did work as designed the kill could be almost instantaneous. They were considered a weapon of last resort if conventional lancing was impossible or a whale was attacking.

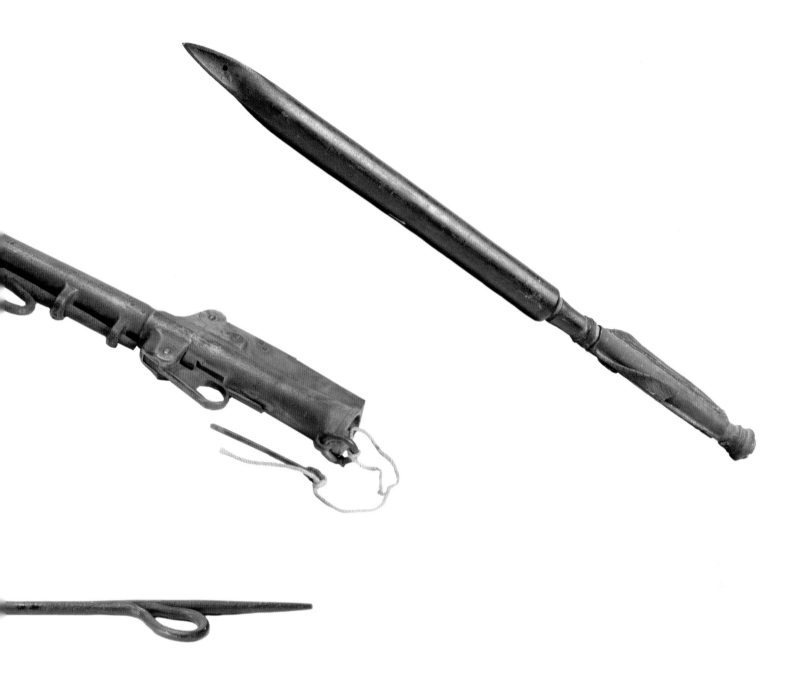

TRACY & BRAND "SWIVEL GUN"

Gosnold Support Center
Nantucket Historical Association

Tracy & Brand of Norwich, Connecticut, also made shoulder-fired weapons. There is no wood on the "pistol stock"—it's all one piece of iron. As the war on whales escalated, a round hole would have been drilled in the bow of the whaleboat to receive the tang of this *very* heavy firearm. A charge of powder and a wad would be rammed deep into the muzzle, followed by a precisely fitted harpoon with the whale line shackled to it. The hammer was cocked back into firing position and a percussion cap was set in place. A mere touch of the trigger would then fire the weapon. The gun could alternately fire a deadly "bomb lance."

TWO WHALE-OIL LAMPS, THREE VIEWS
Wellfleet Historical Society

These tin or galvanized steel lamps are very simple. A cotton wick (or wicks) draws the oil up from the reservoir below. The seams on the lamp with the large single wick are crimped. The seams on the other are soldered. The one lamp has an eccentricly shaped cowl to cover the fill spout. As the cotton wick charred away, it would be advanced with a sharp awl-like tool called a pickwick.

Protective caps hide the wick configuration on the second lamp. Whale oil (especially in the cold) could be thick and resistant to flow up the wick. Scores of patent wick devices, often of brass, tin or pewter, would seek to conduct some of the warmth of the flame back into the pool of oil below. Adjustment of light intensity was simple: if more light were required, you would fire up an additional wick.

CHANDLERY CATALOGUE
Wm. G. Wing & Co., New Bedford
Martha's Vineyard Museum

A chandlery acts as a general store that is capable of carrying almost everything needed on a voyage. Shipowners were savvy business folk and expected good-quality merchandise at fair prices.

The catalogue functioned as both an inventory of available goods as well as an order form. The number of required items would be placed in the left column. The "Do." notation that recurs stands for "Ditto."

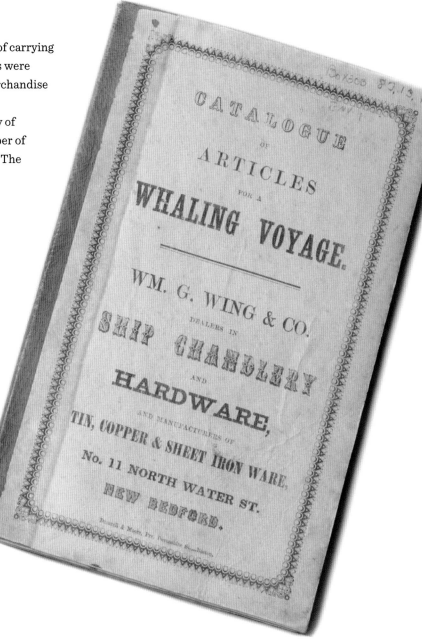

CHANDLERY CATALOGUE, DETAILS
Wm. G. Wing & Co., New Bedford
Martha's Vineyard Museum

The Wing & Co. chandlery clearly wished to accommodate all the shopping needs of the departing vessel. Here in addition to foods, spices and cleaning supplies, under "Medical," they listed New England Rum, Holland Gin, Brandy, etc.

The final item, "Specie," indicates that they were ready and willing to supply precious metals, coins or bullion for the ship's world travel.

Loaf Sugar,
Butter,
Cheese,
Hams,
Smoked Beef,
Codfish,
Mackerel,
Tongues and Sounds.
Old Cider,
Vinegar,
Pickles,
Coffee,
Souchong Tea,
Hyson Tea,
Chocolate,
Raisins,
Black Pepper,
Cayenne Pepper,
Allspice,
Mustard,
Mustard Seed,
Ginger,
Cassia,
Nutmegs,
Cloves,
Saleratus,

Coarse Salt,
Lemon Syrup,
Pepper Sauce,
Sweet Oil,
Essence Spruce,
Hops,
Sage,
Summer Savory,
Hard Soap,
Oil   do.
Lamp Oil,
Sperm Candles,
Corn,
Potatoes,
Onions,
Turnips,

MEDICAL.

New England Rum,
Holland Gin,
Brandy,
Port Wine,
Madeira,
Medicine Chest,
Epsom Salts.

Specie.

Iron Square,
Try   do.
Board Gauge,
Chalk Lines,
Sand Paper,
Whet Stones,
Oil   do.
Sand   do.
Rifle   do.
Sand Rifles,
Tool Handles,
Axe   do.
Anvil,
Bench Vice,
Vice Screws and Boxes,
Hand Vice,
Thumb do.
Screw Plate,
Wrench,
Leaning Knives,
Boat   do.
Pitch Pot,
Butt Cock,
Caulking Mallet,
    do.   Irons,
Making   do.
Marline Spikes,

Hand Cuffs,
Rigging Screws,
Rope Jack,
Flat Files, 14, 13, 12, 11, 10,
    9, 8 inch,
1-2 Round, 14, 13, 12, 11, 10,
    9, 8 inch,
Round, 10, 9, 8, 7, 6, 5,
Saw, 7, 6, 5, 4, 3 inch,
Rasps, flat,
    do.   half round,
Shovels,
Hoes,
Scrapers,
Pricker Pad and Tools,
Brad Awls,
Sewing Awls,
Pegging do.
Shoe Thread,
Fire Steels,
Dust Brushes,
Floor   do.
Paint   do.
Tool   do.
Marking do.
Tar   do.
Scrubbing do.

FLENSING SHOES

Azorean Collection
New Bedford Whaling Museum

These hinged wooden "shoes" with metal studs were strapped on (probably) bare feet before the daring
man was lowered onto the slippery whale carcass that floated alongside the whaleship. He would wear a
sturdy security vest called a monkey jacket. Rope lines were attached to this and held by two men above
him on the narrow "cutting stage."

   His task was to prepare each successive whale for "flensing"—Americans would usually say "cutting
in." He would use a long metal rod called a "head needle" to thread cables and chain into the jawbone. This
chain when winched to the forward part of the ship allowed control over the carcass as the blubber was
removed. A second chain, looped around the "small" near the whale's flukes would be similarly winched
aft. The final task (as blue sharks were usually feasting on the carcass) would be to see that the massive
blubber hook was captured into a hole that had been gouged into the initial flap of dense fat.

Chapter Seven

CUTTING IN

The removal of blubber and other parts of the whale was known in America as "cutting in." In other parts of the world it was known as flensing. For simplicity of explanation we assume a calm sea and further assume that a sperm whale is being worked.

The first cut made in the vanquished whale is usually a hole chopped all the way through the tough, substantial tissue near the whale's flukes, or tail. The whaleboat crew is equipped with a sharp, short-handled boat spade for just that purpose. It allows an initial tow line to be secured to their catch. If any real towing is required, however, the whale is usually tethered to a line attached at the head in order that he be pulled "as he swam"—headfirst.

The dead whale was positioned along the starboard side of the whaleship with the head oriented toward the stern. The "rail" along the starboard side in the "waist" of a whaleship was cut away flush with the deck to facilitate the cutting-in process. A narrow platform of planks was lowered into position over the whale from which the officers handled the actual cutting-in and directed the action. The slices into the whale were made from this cutting stage with ultrasharp spades attached to slender poles 16 to 20 feet long. Usually, the boatsteerer who planted the harpoon that began the catch has the "honor" of being lowered over the side onto the heaving, slippery surface of the whale's back or side. From there he fastens the initial hooks, lines and sinkers to the whale's body for the cutting and carving to follow.

On the open ocean hundreds of 6- or 7-foot blue sharks made a banquet of the corpse. Clustered like maggots, they snarled away mouthfuls of blubber and flesh just inches from the boatsteerer's bare feet.

The animal was secured with one chain fastened to the bony area of the head and a second around the "small" of his tail so that he could be repeatedly turned longitudinally like a spindle. A pair of initial scarfed cuts were made into the blubber from a position just aft of the whale's eye. As the blubber was separated from the flesh, a hole was chopped into this 3-foot-wide slab in order to receive the hundredweight "blubber hook" which was hefted on powerful blocks and tackle. All hands strained at the winches to wrest away the animal's thick jacket of blubber. What was made was essentially one continuous spiral cut (like skinning the peel off a lemon in one coil). But, in fact, a second hook was brought into play as manageable blanket pieces (each weighing tons) were slashed free, brought aboard and stored skin-down in a temporary hold, the blubber room, or blubber parlor.

The head of a sperm whale was very carefully removed in its entirety. If the whale (which might measure anywhere from 40 to 60 feet in length) was of a manageable size relative to the ship, the specific head parts were further separated and hefted onto the deck. Even the lower jaw with its ivory-like teeth was hoisted onto the deck. The most valuable portion of the entire whale was contained in this head matter: the case was an enclosed, fibrous reservoir containing numerous barrels of spermaceti. This snow-white, silky liquid would be carefully collected and set apart for separate processing and storage. A barrel of spermaceti would command a price several times higher than even the finest sperm oil rendered from the blubber.

SWEEPING AND FLUKING

The operations of bringing a dead whale alongside the ship, and of attaching it, are called sweeping and fluking. After the line from the carcass has been passed onboard, a heavy chain, made fast around a bitt on the forward deck, is paid out through the starboard hawse pipe. A light rope is then dipped under the whale's "small" (the tail end, just in front of the flukes), and is used in turn to pull the chain around. As soon as the slack has been drawn in, the whale floats on the starboard side of the ship, with its flukes toward the bow and its head stretching along past the waist. The process is simple enough in quiet weather, but today there has been a small choppy sea and the fluking was accomplished only with a good deal of hard labor by the crew and of still harder language by the Old Man.

As soon as our prizes were safe alongside, the fall blocks were dropped to the four boats and all hands laid hold and swayed back until the precious craft were triced up into position on the cranes, the salt water streaming from plug holes in their bottoms. Then it was "Supper the watch," and nobody needed urging to a meal so long overdue.

As darkness closed in, the nearest whale lay on its side, fin out, limberly yielding to every swell, with its great blunt head stretching toward the quarter and its closed eye and infinitesimal ear-opening occasionally breaking above the surface. I could still see the troop of hungry sharks filing silently along its length, fondly rubbing tail fins against the gray hulk, as though they were anticipating the feast of the cutting-in.

August 19. We lay hove-to throughout a night that grew calmer as the hours passed.

At half past four o'clock this morning, every soul was on deck and on duty. My only job, however, was to sit at some good point of vantage, such as the mate's boat on the starboard quarter, and watch proceedings.

In the dim light of early dawn, two pieces of apparatus were immediately brought into use—one the cutting tackle, the other the cutting stage. The latter is a scaffold which, when lowered from the ship's waist, is suspended directly above the whale. On this rocking platform the officers stand while performing the cutting-in. The cutting tackle is a cluster of enormous blocks hung, by hawsers as thick as a man's leg, from the head of the mainmast, the strongest structure on a ship above the deck. Through these blocks are rove the hawsers which lift many tons of blubber from the water to the main hatch.

A great iron hook, weighing about a hundred pounds, was lowered from the cutting tackle and inserted in a prepared gash in the blubber just behind the sperm whale's eye. This was accomplished easily this morning because of the quietness of the sea, and tension applied to the line at once raised the carcass high in the water. Then the officers, leaning against the rail to steady themselves, began to cut a flap of blubber around the inserted hook, using for this purpose razor-edged blubber spades, which have handles fifteen or twenty feet long.

In the brightening morning, the officers jabbed and jabbed from the stage, sometimes seeing where they struck, and sometimes, when the whale was engulfed in boiling foam, only guessing. Their spades dulled rapidly, and on the quarterdeck, with the laziest Portugee on board to turn the grindstone, my friend Correia, the cooper, was kept busy renewing edges until the last cut had been concluded. "Sharp spade, Cooper!" the four officers were continually bawling out from the stage, while the cooper cursed under his breath at their recklessness in chipping the spades against bones or a harpoon imbedded in the blubber.

On the deck of the *Daisy*, at the other end of the cutting tackle, no less heavy work was going on. Double hawsers ran through the great blocks to the windlass on the topgallant fo'c's'le, and there, under the eye of the Old Man himself, the greater part of the crew rocked the windlass and hoisted the strip of blubber as it was loosened from the whale. This was at least the cheery part of the business, work that could not be done without song, and, to the accompaniment of squeaking bearings and clicking pawls, the husky chorus rang out:

> *Come all ye brave sailors who're cruising for sparm,*
> *Come all ye bold seamen who sail round the Horn—*
> *Our Captain has told us, and we hope it proves true,*
> *There's plenty more whales 'long the coast of Peru.*

Back at the waist, the stress of the windlass soon began to rip the first strip of blubber from the whale's body. Scrambling sharks made the water crawl as each fish tried to bury its teeth in exposed fat. Now and then a shark would flounder right out of the water, on top of the whale, until a descending blubber spade put an end to its ambitions.

Eventually, the windlass grinders pulled up the strip of blubber until the paired blocks of the tackle were almost in contact, high above the main deck, block-a-block, the long, tough blanket-piece of skin and fat hanging from that point to its attachment on the whale, which had rolled over and over in the water as its blubber had been peeled off along the scarf. The jabbing of the spades went on incessantly, and the water for an acre around the brig was stained by outpouring blood.

When the blanket-piece had been hoisted higher and higher, until it could rise no further, the third mate, armed with a long-handled double-edged sword called the boarding knife, cut a pair of holes through the blubber down near the level of the deck. A chain looped in and out of these was connected with a second hawser, the "port-falls" of the cutting blocks. When this new attachment had been drawn taut on the windlass, the boarding knife slashed through the blubber just above it. The upper piece swung free across the deck, to the peril of anyone who chanced to be in its path, but it was soon controlled and lowered down the main hatch into the slithery blubber parlor, where men with short-handled spades reduced it to mincing pieces that could be stowed in pens.

Then the second blanket piece hung in the gory sea, the chain which held it grinding on the plank-sheer of the waist, and the identical procedure was repeated until this, too, rose dripping over the deck, ready to be severed. And so on, down to the small of the whale, which was cut through and hoisted aboard, flukes and all.

Before the stripped carcass was set adrift, the intestines were well punched with the long spades, and the officers smelled their blades with the unrealized hope of detecting ambergris. Most of the sharks, squirming like massed maggots, went off with the carcass, which floated high as a result of eighteen hours' decomposition.

CUTTING IN

AUGUST 22, 1912

Within a very brief time and before I had even arrived on deck, two of them [boats] harpooned and lanced an eighty-barrel bull, a sperm whale which makes his predecessors seem insignificant and which will, indeed, yield much more oil than all four of them together. As the creature floated alongside, I measured its extreme length, between markers on the *Daisy*'s deck, as 55 feet 10 inches, which is certainly accurate to within less than one foot.

Most of the sharks were patient, so to speak, swimming slowly along the whale and around the brig, an exceedingly interesting though somewhat macabre procession. They were slender and swift-looking creatures, of an intense blue color on the upper surface of the body, with small but conspicuous teeth, and of an average—and remarkably uniform—length of about eight feet. The species is the common surface shark of the high sea in the tropical and subtropical Atlantic, and is rarely seen near the continental coasts.

The sharks evidently lost their aforementioned patience, for during the dark hours they scooped many neat mouthfuls of blubber out of the whale, leaving white gouges in the blackskin. When the blubber spades recommenced their work, with a new reddening of the water, the sharks went berserk. Many of them jumped or wriggled on top of the whale, where they were methodically chopped to pieces by the officers on the cutting stage. Some were washed back into deep water badly mutilated but still able to swim, and these, even though their entrails were hanging out of the side of a body that had been cut away, would turn again toward the whale, bury their teeth, twist, yank, and swallow. I believe, though I am not quite certain, that one or more of these insensate fish were taking food in the mouth and immediately losing it through a stomach that had been severed by a blubber spade. At any rate, the hacked-up brutes continued to feed until they died in the act and slowly settled into impenetrable depths beneath our keel.

Our former whales all being small, their heads were hoisted on deck entire. Then the "case" (the top section of the head which contains the spermaceti) was cautiously slit open, and the limpid, fragrant spermaceti, mingled with stringy masses of snow-white fat, was bailed out with copper scoops and poured into tubs.

The head of a whale like the bull now alongside weighs many tons, for a sperm whale's head is reckoned as a third of the total length and more than a third of the bulk. The strain of such a head hanging from the blocks of the cutting tackle would be liable to break the hawsers, or even to force the foot of the mast through the keel and thus to scuttle the ship. So the head of a big whale must be handled quite differently from that of a small one.

This morning Captain Cleveland himself came for the first time out on the cutting stage. Working only with Mr. da Lomba [the 1st mate], after the stripping of the body blubber had been nearly completed, he cut transversely into the enormous mass of tissue, presently exposing the condyles of the vast skull and finally decapitating the whale. The head was then attached by a line to the lash-rail and allowed to float aft until the swollen, grisly carcass was cut adrift.

Next, the entire fore and upper part of the whale's head, comprising not only the case but also a huge mass of fat called the junk, was severed from the skull. After that, case and junk were in turn separated one from the other by cutting cautiously through a fibrous layer known as the "Whitehorse," which forms a sort of floor for the case. The junk was then hoisted on deck, to be chopped subsequently into oleaginous blocks and fed into the trypots. The great cistern of the case, with its hundreds of gallons of spermaceti inside, remained floating in the sea.

At this point, José Gaspar, one of the boatsteerers, volunteered to go overboard to make the fastenings. (It seems that the boatsteerers always volunteer for this job—but each in his own turn!) Girdled with a monkey-belt of braided marlin, from which a tether ran to competent hands on deck, José was lowered into the seething water. By timely yanks on the rope, he was kept from being squeezed between case and ship as they rolled together in the swell. On the cutting stage the officers stood with their long spades, sending one shark after another to Davy Jones's locker while the poor boatsteerer, now thrown high, now half drowned in foam and froth, completed his task of sewing a sort of spiderweb of cordage around the rear end of the case in order to form an attachment for a heavy line from the cutting blocks. This delicate bit of tailoring was accomplished with a "head needle" about two feet long. Finally the job was fulfilled, and José was hauled and bumped to the deck.

The hinder end of the case was then hoisted level with the planksheer of the waist. Its weight was supported more by water than by our cutting tackle, for the snout was still far beneath the surface. Mr. da Lomba then used a short-handled spade to tap the store of spermaceti from above, i.e., from the back of the case, exercising great care not to spill any of it. A few cupfuls that gushed on deck were promptly scooped up by slick-skimmers, meaning anybody standing by and not already fully occupied.

Then, through a light tackle hung from the tip of the foresail yard, a long, narrow, round-bottomed case bucket, suspended at the end of a thin pole, was lowered through the slit that had just been made in the case. The pole was used to push the bucket in, and then to haul it out again, as from a well, filled to the brim and dripping with liquid spermaceti. This operation was repeated again and again, until the long pole rammed the "old oaken bucket" down fifteen or twenty feet, and drained the last few gallons. All of this luscious and valuable spermaceti was poured into butts and tubs, to be boiled separately from the body blubber. Finally, the great sack, emptied of its treasure, was cut away to plunge into the deep. The last of the fat was now on board; the drainage oil and spilth were "likkered up" from the slippery decks; the stage was raised to its inactive position, and the cutting-in was over.

The Lower Jaw

The lower jaw of the eighty-barrel sperm whale was the first one we have saved. After the great masses of lush fat had been taken out of the ramus, or pan, on either side, it was roughly trimmed up but the fifty teeth were left in place. When the boiling of blubber had been completed, the gear stowed, and the brig cleaned up, this jaw was lowered into the ocean and towed astern for several days at the end of a long length of whale line. It was astonishing to see how clean and white it became in the tropical water, all the oil evidently being washed out of it and all the clinging meat macerated by the warmth or devoured by tiny organisms. Before the gristle, which held the teeth in their sockets, had softened too much, the jaw was once more hoisted on deck and lashed to the bulwarks near the bow. Later in the voyage the white bone of this jaw, and the creamy ivory of the great teeth, will no doubt be worked into scrimshaw by the officers.

SPADE FOR CUTTING IN
Cold Spring Harbor Whaling Museum

This cast-steel cutting spade would be fitted with a wooden pole and secured with a nail, screw or pin to keep it in place. The curved forward edge would be kept as sharp as a woodsman's axe. When used for stripping blubber from the "cutting stage," the tool and handle could be from 16 to 20 feet long. This same tool could be fitted with a medium-length handle and used as a "deck spade." The whaleboat always carried a shorter-handled spade. This could have been a "gouge spade" with a curved, shovel shape to pierce a circular hole through a substantial part of the carcass (usually near the flukes) so that an initial tow line could be attached to the prize. Spades came in a whole range of shapes and sizes to suit particular tasks.

ENGRAVING, *IMPLEMENTS USED IN CUTTING IN A WHALE*
Book Illustration

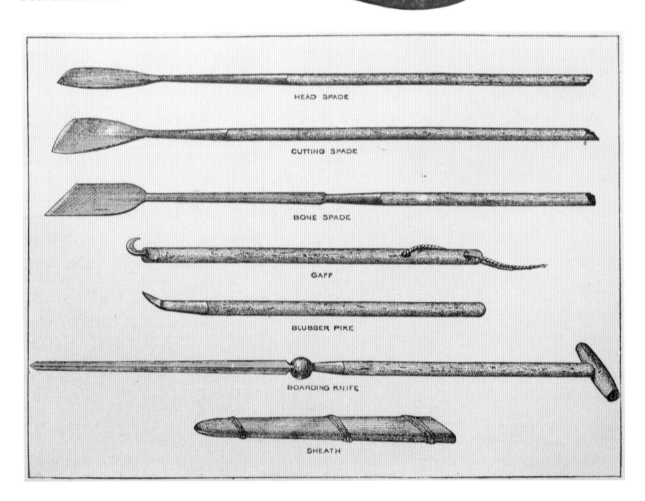

HEAD SPADE

CUTTING SPADE

BONE SPADE

GAFF

BLUBBER PIKE

BOARDING KNIFE

SHEATH

BLUBBER HOOK
Gosnold Support Center
Nantucket Historical Association

This cast-iron hook is smaller and less heavy-duty than the primary hook, but otherwise identical. The small eyelet hole that has been punched at the bend of the J would accept a shackle with rope attached. The main shackle that is permanently pinned at the top of the hook took the strain of the blanket piece being hoisted. The line attached at the hole would allow a hand working on deck to guide the massive slab being "boarded" to a point where it could be lowered through the hatch leading to the blubber parlor.

The whale is being worked along the port side of the vessel. The cutting stage and deck configuration would normally be set to the starboard side.

If the seas were up, the vessel could be turned so that the work could be done on the lee side. In very rough weather, a good deal of slack would be given to the chained and tethered carcass to keep it from ripping at the ship's timbers.

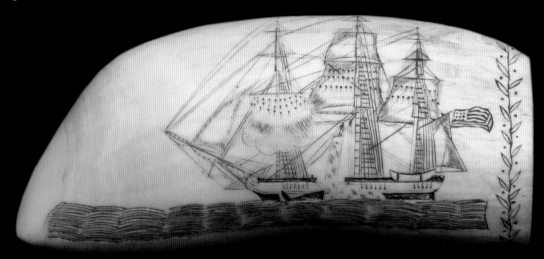

ENGRAVING, *DIAGRAM SHOWING THE MANNER OF CUTTING-IN THE BOWHEAD AND RIGHT WHALE*

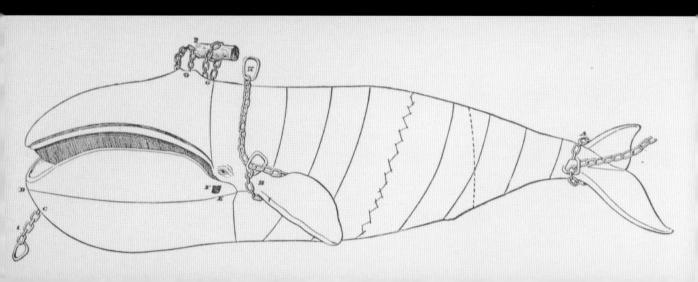

BOOK ENGRAVING, *CUTTING IN A WHALE*

Engraved by Rouarque in 1850

Here, we are looking at the starboard side of a rather small vessel. The whale is riding unnaturally high in the water, although the strain from the blubber-hook tackle could be causing some of that. The workers with the long cutting spades on deck are far closer to the animal than one might expect on a larger vessel with more freeboard. The whale's head faces the vessel's stern. The fluke chains near the whale's tail are secured through the hawseholes near the bow. These chains will be constantly adjusted as the scarfed piece of blubber is drawn up and the floating carcass needs to be "rolled." The workers at the far right are pumping at the windlass handles. This slowly reels in the "falls"—the lines raising the blubber-hook tackles.

ENGRAVING, *OUTLINE OF A SPERM WHALE, SHOWING THE MANNER OF CUTTING-IN*

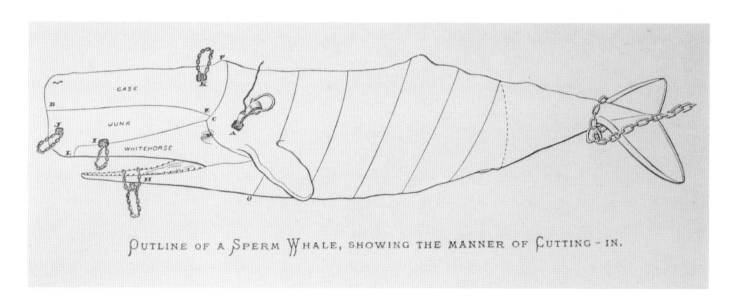

OUTLINE OF A SPERM WHALE, SHOWING THE MANNER OF CUTTING-IN.

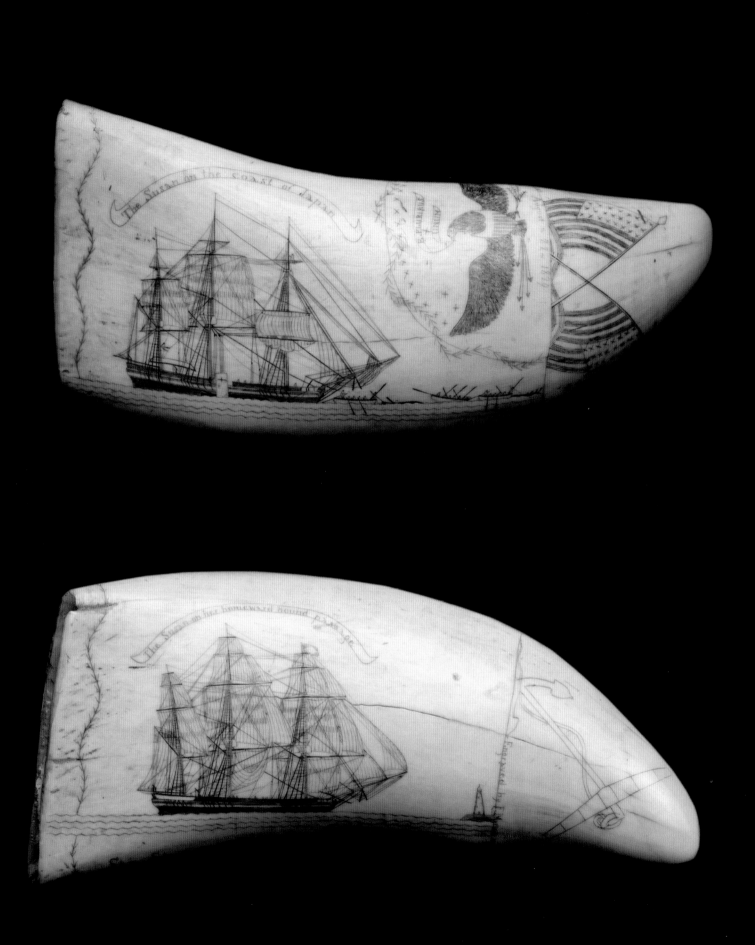

"GREASY LUCK" TOOTH SHOWING THE SHIP *SUSAN*, FOUR VIEWS
Nantucket Whaling Museum

The artist makes efficient use of all the "real estate" to cover this tooth with designs and written text. First, he adds a hairline border near the tip, which coincides with the yellowed portion that would have protruded through the whale's gum line. He decorates this area with crossed American flags and an anchor. One broad surface is decorated with the ship under sail and the other side shows "The Susan on the Coast of Japan," a patriotic eagle and boats lowered for hunting. A blanket piece of blubber hangs as if cutting in had been interrupted by an order to lower boats for more hunting.

One narrow side is inscribed "Ship Susan of Nantucket—Frederick Swain—Master." The other narrow edge has the following "toast":

Death to the living—long life to the killers.
Success to sailor's wives & greasy luck to whalers.

"Greasy luck!" or "Have a greasy v'yage" was a common farewell as a ship was leaving Nantucket.

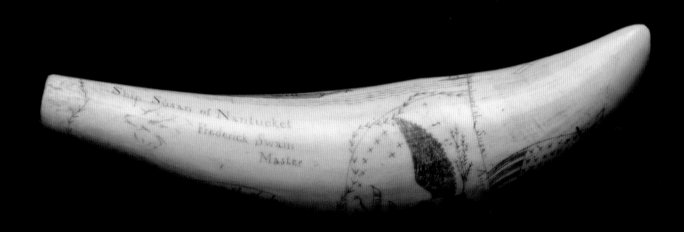

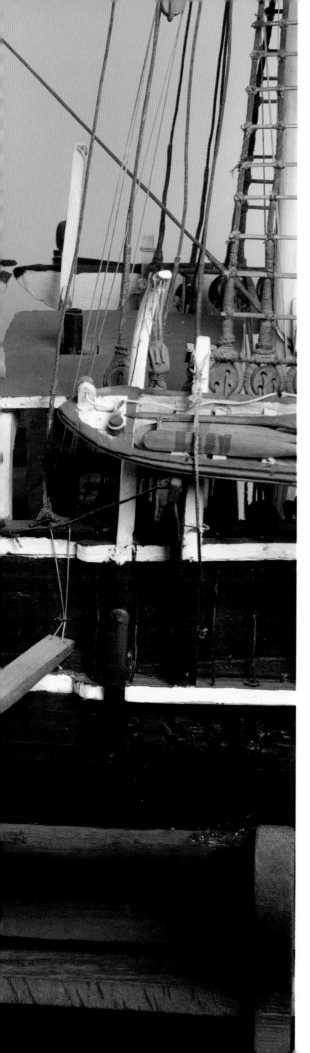

SAILOR-BUILT MODEL OF THE WHALESHIP
CHARLES W. MORGAN
Gosnold Support Center
Nantucket Historical Association

In spite of a bit of roughness and lack of finesse, this model has a great deal of charm and attention to detail. We see that just two whaleboats hang from this starboard side to allow for the narrow-planked cutting stage, which is cantilevered out in position for the cutting-in of captured whales.

COVERED SECTION OF THE WEATHER DECK
Whaleship Charles W. Morgan
Mystic Seaport

An assortment of whalecraft can be seen stowed in a rack above the work area. In addition to the cutting spades, a harpoon and a lance are seen. This area is quite near the starboard waist of the vessel where the cutting stage is erected. The unpainted wood construction in the background is a sturdy (but temporary) covering that supports clear plastic waterproofing so that renovation work on the ship can carry on in all weather. On a whaling cruise a spare whaleboat or two might be lashed to the top of this "roof."

PAINTING—SHIP *SPERMO*

Nantucket Whaling Museum

"Ship *Spermo* Trying With Boats Among Whales On California—1821."

The ship is "under way" in heavy weather with the trypots ablaze. Still, boats have been lowered since more whales might be taken. Two prior kills float low in the water to the right. Each is marked with a "waif"—in this case a black circle attached to a stake.

Chapter Eight

TRYING OUT

Each prize whale brought alongside the ship will require days of rank, intense, greasy, hot, slippery labor. The yield will be tons of oil ready for market. Since all on board were working for a share of the proceeds, they knew that every barrel of oil stowed away was money in their pocket. It also meant that the sooner the holds were filled with oil, the sooner they'd head for home.

The head of a sperm whale, as described earlier, often got the immediate attention, but the trying-out process whereby the blubber is boiled to release its oil was generally the same process no matter what type of whale was being worked.

The blubber had previously been crowded into the blubber parlor. Two greenies were usually given the duty of getting down through the hatch and slicing the blanket pieces into more manageable horse pieces, which when flopped up onto the deck could be slid around with metal hooks.

The workers on deck would get these pieces to a cutting table (the mincing horse), where they were further reduced in size. The mincing knife, a curved blade with a handle at each end, deftly cut the blubber into 1-foot cubes and then into ¼-inch slabs. These bacon-like strips were kept attached, along one edge usually on the skin side, like pages of a bound book, perhaps the "good book." These "bible pieces" were kept in a hopper ready to be fed into the heated iron kettles. As they became crispy brown and had given up most of their locked-in oil, they were removed with a hook or fork and tossed into a separate hopper. They would be drained of their oil before being put aside as "scrap." The initial tryworks fire was started with precious firewood, but soon scrap alone was the only fuel needed to cook the blubber. It was well capable of providing the intense, even heat.

Notwithstanding the smoke, the soot and the filth attendant to the trying-out process, the oil was watched and coddled with laboratory precision. Solids were kept from burning at the bottom of the kettle, lest the oil darken or change consistency. Several days were allowed for the oil to cool gently. Every care was taken to insure that what was finally sealed shut in the wooden casks would command the highest market price.

No matter if whales were being taken one at a time or several taken in a short period of time, a thorough cleanup followed. The decks were scrubbed clean. The soot clinging to the sails and rigging—being potash—was collected. This alkaline substance when mixed with water was employed as a cleaning agent. All of the equipment was made spotless. Men climbed into the great 350-gallon cauldrons and used sand as an abrasive to scour the insides to a shining brightness. The "round-the-clock" clothes they wore, having been saturated with the oil, soot and gurry, were cleansed anew. Finally, the men themselves did their best to clean themselves from head to toe. A rain shower after several days of trying out was particularly welcome.

Excerpt from Logbook for Grace *by Robert Cushman Murphy*

(1887–1973)

FIERY TRYPOTS AT NIGHT

October 3, 1912

If there is any modern counterpart of an uncouth revel around a witches' brew, it is the scene of the trypots at night.

It was eight bells (midnight) when we had cut-in the final fish. The *Daisy*, with topsails aback, rolled gently in the quiet swell, while the officers on the cutting stage punched with their spades as best they could in the dismal light of lanterns and oil-soaked torches. The flickering glare showed the hulk of the whale alongside and the flash of bloody wavelets beyond. On deck a cresset, or bug light, of burning blubber scrap, and the fiery chimneys of the tryworks in full blast, cast enough illumination to reveal the great blankets of blubber and the greasy, toiling figures scurrying about amid the shouting of orders, the creak of tackles and the clank of chains. At six bells the last strip came over the planksheer. The severed head of the whale floated by the starboard quarter, lashed securely and ready to be handled at daybreak. Only the rite of the whaleman's ultimate hope remained to be carried out before the flensed carcass should be cut adrift.

The Old Man joined his officers on the cutting stage. Then, with methodical movements, he and the three mates thrust freshly sharpened cutting spades deeply into the guts of the whale, twisted them, cautiously withdrew them, smelled the bright steel blades, and scrutinized them painstakingly in the glow of a lantern, while the crew looked on in fevered anticipation. Back and forth along the stage the four men trod and jabbed, until the vitals had been intimately explored. But nary a whiff of the longed-for odor of ambergris was forthcoming. "And so to bed."

Excerpt from Logbook for Grace *by Robert Cushman Murphy*

(1887–1973)

DESCRIPTION OF
BLUBBER PROCESSING

After blubber is hoisted aboard until the main deck presents a discouraging appearance, heaped up with the overflow of the blubber room; after one or more carcasses have been cut adrift, and the spermaceti has been bailed from the cases; after every member of the crew is at the point of collapse from hustling, hauling, chopping, lashing, stowing, rocking the windlass, and slipping galley-west on the greasy planks—then you are ready to mince and boil. Some skippers have a pleasant interlude between cutting-in and cooking. It is known as splicing the main brace, which means that each sweaty man files to the quarterdeck and gulps down a tot of rum. But no such happy custom prevails on the *Daisy*. The Old Man believes that there is already far too much drinking and profanity in the world.

The blanket pieces, above and below deck, are cut into "horse pieces," which are flitches about two feet long and a little wider than the thickness of the blubber. These are handled with two-pronged blubber forks and are heaped along the port rail, ready for mincing. The strips are minced before boiling so that the heat may penetrate every portion of the fat and extract all the oil. Mincing is accomplished with a huge double-handled drawknife. One man, holding a meat hook, pushes horse pieces along a table, while another slashes across and back with the drawknife, cutting the strip into thin slices. These, however, are not completely severed, but are left clinging together, like bacon on the rind, so that the whole strip—now called a "bible"—can be manipulated on a blubber fork.

The bibles are boiled in the tryworks on the forward deck, which consists of an enormous pair of iron pots in a brick support and firebox, the latter being insulated from the wooden deck by a water bath. Beside the tryworks stands the cooler, a rectangular iron tank into which the oil is ladled from the pots.

The blubber is boiled until the minced strips, crisp, shriveled, and of a golden brown color, rise to the bubbling surface, where they float like clinkers. They then constitute the scrap, which is the fuel of this self-supporting process. The boiled-out blubber of one victim is used to cook the next one. The bits of scrap are pitched off the pots, after a momentary drainage, and are subsequently fed to the fires beneath, burning with an avid and roaring flame, and leaving almost no ash.

After the boiled oil, now of a beautiful amber hue, has been passed through the cooler to the storage tank between decks, the ship gets once more under way, the lookouts mount to their perches, the decks are scoured, the rigging cleaned of its accumulation of grease and soot, and the watch, with the cooper in charge, runs the oil through a canvas hose into the bungs of the great casks. From the quarterdeck the Old Man, looking very sour—as he unvaryingly does when he is happiest—casts his weather eye aloft and orders the mastheads to look sharp and raise another whale. And everybody longs for a repetition of the hard labor because, after all, every barrel of oil is a barrel nearer a full ship and homeward bound.

WHALE OIL AND BLACKFISH OIL
Photographed Outside the Wellfleet Historical Society Museum

The larger bottle with the amber fluid is simply labeled "whale oil." In the trade that was one way of indicating "not sperm oil." Over the decades part of the oil has congealed into a thready, cobweb shape.

The smaller sample is labeled "blackfish oil." The oil's clear color is indicative of its purity. It has desirable lubricating properties and was valued by machinists, watchmakers and makers of precision instruments. Blackfish is another name for the pilot whale, which frequently gets stranded on the sandy shoals of Cape Cod Bay near Wellfleet. It's about the same size as its relative the orca or killer whale—20 to 25 feet. It has a prominent bulb atop its head that yields a quantity of high-quality, clear oil. It required little, if any, processing. Wellfleet has a small tidal stream called Blackfish Creek.

Local history records an enormous stranding of some 1,500 pilot whales in 1885. Scores of local men were able to "drive" them like cattle into the salt marshes so that they could be harvested as the tide retreated. Each adult whale yielded about one barrel (30.5 gallons) of excellent oil. The entire quantity was sold at market for $14,000 and the proceeds were divided among the workers.

CAST-IRON TRYPOT, TWO VIEWS
Nantucket Whaling Museum

A large trypot such as this could weigh well over 1,000 pounds. Its lip would measure almost 60 inches from the floor. The flat side allowed two pots to be placed snugly together in the bricked-in firebox. The larger pots such as this had a capacity of 220 gallons. Two of them working in tandem would contain the equivalent of fourteen barrels of oil (a barrel was set at 30.5 gallons). There was a foundry in New Bedford that supplied trypots in varying sizes. The handles were part of the "single-pour" casting and facilitated the movement of the pot, when necessary. The vertical seam near the handles is not a weld but a "mold mark" showing where two halves came together prior to the pour of molten iron. This pot has three cast legs, which raised the kettle above the brick firebox floor.

The inside of the pot was expected to "glisten like polished silver" before the blubber-rendering operation commenced. A man would climb inside with a scouring abrasive as simple as sand and polish away any rust or scale from previous uses. The "product" would be tested, rated, graded and assayed before a price was offered at the market. Any adulterant, contaminant or evidence of poor handling could dramatically lower the oil's value. The pots would usually have a sheet-metal cover when idle. Men, when idle, were known to climb in and curl up for a snooze.

SPERM OIL

Robeco Chemical Co., New York
Cold Spring Harbor Whaling Museum

Pharmacists and chemical suppliers frequently use brown glass or opaque containers for sensitive products. Sunlight and other bright light could cause sperm oil to darken or lose viscosity.

MECCA SPERM OIL

Mecca Paint & Varnish Co., Long Island City, New York
Cold Spring Harbor Whaling Museum

Here we have a consumer product that is likely to have been packaged exactly as processed aboard the whaleship with no further refinement or additives.

Long Island City is in the borough of Queens—situated between Brooklyn and the Bronx—just across the East River from Manhattan. It's ironic that the brand name Mecca is also the name of the city in oil-rich Saudi Arabia. Oil pumped from the ground is filling virtually all of the needs formerly satisfied by whale oil. Oil-based paint is an example. Petroleum, or "fossil oil," has also come to be recognized as a finite resource.

WHALE-OIL SOAP

Cold Spring Harbor Whaling Museum

The wrapper states: "For Destroying Insects on Plants and Trees." It would seem to be a bit harsh for everyday human bathing. There were, however, scores of cosmetic uses for whale oil.

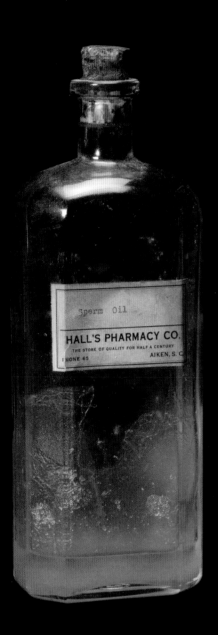

Hall's Pharmacy, Aiken, South Carolina
Cold Spring Harbor Whaling Museum

This is obviously an early-twentieth-century product. Note that the phone number contains but two digits.

BOTTLE OF "CRUDE SPERM WHALE OIL"
Cold Spring Harbor Whaling Museum

This looks as if it has been bottled and labeled for museum or display purposes. All of the sperm whale oil extracted from blubber contains particles of spermaceti oil, which is found concentrated and in its purest form in the huge membrane (sac) in the head. That oil was collected and stored separately. It required virtually no rendering. Still, crude sperm whale oil was of a finer quality and commanded a higher price than the oil extracted from the blubber of other hunted whales. We can see here that the unprocessed oil has separated into two strata.

NYE OIL
Cold Spring Harbor Whaling Museum

Nye is a well-known name in Yankee whaling. The Nye family included shipowners and tradesmen in all facets of whaling. They distributed a high-quality lubricant for home use as well as specialty lubricants for sewing machines and other precision equipment.

BLOCK OF PRESSED SPERMACETI WAX
Sag Harbor Whaling Museum

The very valuable spermaceti "oil" found in abundance in a reservoir in the head of a sperm whale is more correctly described as a wax. The elaborate process for extracting and solidifying this wax on a commercial scale (mainly for the manufacture of candles) was a closely guarded secret on Nantucket for many years.

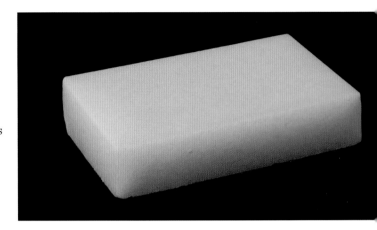

NANTUCKET SPERMACETI PRESS
Old Candle Factory
Nantucket Whaling Museum

Imagine the mechanics of a garlic press or a nutcracker. Such tools are frequently hinged at the very end and have handles that can be squeezed together for leverage. The same principle is at work here but on a massive scale. One "handle" is a timber post 14 inches square and 30 feet long.

    Sperm oil has already been strained and filtered to concentrate the waxy solids (stearates). That thick concoction is poured into a tightly woven woolen bag about the size of a bedroom pillow. It is placed on a solid platen, and the leverage is applied causing the lighter oil to ooze out through the weave in the bag. A trough collects the still-valuable lighter oil. With a bit more processing the spermaceti wax solids collected in the bag were made into candles. Unlike tallow candles they were smokeless and odor-free. They burned slowly with a bright, clear light.

METAL STENCIL
"BLEACHED WINTER SPERM OIL"

Nantucket Candle Factory

Nantucket Whaling Museum

The liquid by-product of the candlemaking was by no means waste. In fact, it represented a high degree of refinement. The cold Nantucket winter air helped to congeal the oil before "pressing." The oil from spermaceti pressed in the winter months was labeled and marketed as a specialty.

BARREL OF SPERMACETI

Gosnold Support Center

Nantucket Historical Association

Here we have it. This is the prize that launched a thousand ships. This blue plastic barrel currently sits in the corner of an out-of-the-way, air-conditioned storage room on Nantucket. It was harvested from a dead sperm whale that washed ashore on that island.

The word *sperma* is Greek for "seed," and *cetus* is Latin for "whale." It was originally thought that the substance found in abundance in the whale's head was his sperm. Current thought holds that the reservoir of spermaceti is used for echolocation. The whale searches for food at great depths.

BRICKS OF SPERMACETI WAX

Martha's Vineyard Museum

Like two pieces of a puzzle, these samples seem to have formerly been one. One was apparently wrapped or stored differently from its "mate," as can be seen from the discoloration. The original products made from spermaceti wax were primarily candles. They would have been bleached to a snowy white and would have burned with a bright flame with almost no smoke or odor.

RECEIPT FOR SHIP-TO-SHIP TRANSPORT OF OIL
Honolulu, Sandwich Islands, 1867

This simple handwritten document acknowledges the transfer of 156 "packages" of whale oil from one New Bedford ship, the *St. George*, to another of the same port, the *Roman*. That cargo totals 29,489 gallons. Also transferred was a single "tank" containing 1,994 gallons of whale oil in "good order and condition."

Lahaina on the island of Maui evolved into the "capital" of Pacific whaling. It was known as a "little New Bedford." Whalers were well aware of the productive "seasons" at the various whaling grounds and they would tie up there to repair, refit and sometimes (as we see here in this Honolulu transaction) off-load their cargo so that they could head out again with an empty ship. Certain ships did no hunting, but acted as "tankers," taking the cargo past Cape Horn and back to the east coast of the United States or even directly to markets around the world.

Honolulu, S. I.,
Nov. 21st 1867

Received on board Ship Roman of new bedford from Ship St. George of new bedford (156) one hundred and fiftysix packages containing (29489) twenty nine thousand four hundred eighty nine gallons of whale oil marked J.P. and dimond and branded Ship St. George also one tank containing (1994) one thousand nine hundred and ninety four gallons of whale oil the same being in good order and condition

H C Borden 1st officer

FUNNEL-STRAINER
Whaleship Charles W. Morgan
Mystic Seaport

The blubber being processed would begin to release its oil as heat was applied. When the liquid reached over 300 degrees, it would boil and give up any trapped water. Just enough heat was applied to "stabilize" the animal fat, which is to say prevent "rot" or rapid decomposition. The book, or bible, pieces had released most of their oil, but still, they were lifted with a fork, allowed to drain over the trypot, and then placed in a tub for additional drainage. *That* oil was saved and the crispy remains became scrap, the highly combustible fuel that fired the kettles. Perforated "skimmers" were constantly worked across the boiling oil to remove solids.

The rendered oil was removed from the pots and set in large cooling tubs. Several days might pass before it was felt that the oil had sufficiently cooled to be piped to large wooden casks waiting below.

This funnel with a perforated screen built in indicates the care involved in processing the hard-won oil. Not a drop was wasted and not a speck of contaminant was tolerated.

BACKSIDE VIEW OF THE TRYWORKS
Whaleship Charles W. Morgan
Mystic Seaport

The rectangular opening in the bricks (surrounded by metal strapping) receives the chimney-smokestack apparatus, which can quickly be mounted or stowed out of the way.

 The two cavernous holes conceal the two trypots. A sheet-metal surface above the pots assures that drips and other morsels of blubber will drain back into the kettles. Sperm whale oil has a reputation as the most highly refined of all the naturally occurring animal fats. It is rated as superior to that of pork, beef, goose or duck. A Mrs. Penniman, a whaler's wife from Eastham, Massachusetts, would accompany her husband on his cruises. When the first sperm whale of the voyage was being "tried out" she would drop doughnut rings into the boiling cauldron as a treat for the crew.

FIREBOX BELOW THE TRYWORKS KETTLES
Whaleship Charles W. Morgan
Mystic Seaport

The hanging iron door can be pushed aside to tend to the fire. Initially, wood is added here to kindle what will eventually be a scrap-fueled fire. Scrap was the name given to crisp clumps of the solids from previously rendered blubber. It had given up all of the recoverable oil but still had the ability to burn with great heat. There is a narrow "hearth"—just the length of one brick.

 Needless to say, fire prevention is a prime concern to all those at sea—especially on a wooden ship with cloth sails and a flammable cargo. The brick portion of the tryworks was specially assembled by a master mason before setting out on a cruise. The design involved a shallow area below the brick firebox, which would hold a jacket of seawater—much as a "radiator" in an internal combustion engine uses water to draw away heat.

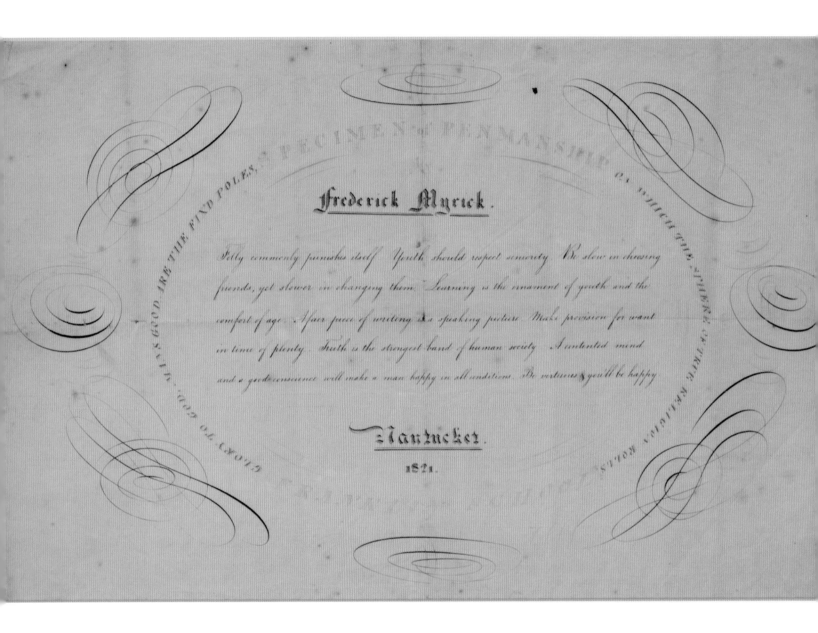

FREDERICK MYRICK (CELEBRATED SCRIMSHANDER)
EARLY PENMANSHIP SAMPLER

Nantucket Whaling Museum

Chapter Nine

LIFE ABOARD

Life aboard a whaler was very different from a life lived on land. It was *vastly* different from life on a merchantman or a naval vessel as well. The men were living in a mobile slaughterhouse. Among the younger men, slight attention was paid to traditional seamanship and shipboard disciplines. Perfectly competent and experienced whalemen would be routinely passed over if they sought to ship on anything but another whaler.

Those with the lowest status aboard were the foremast hands. They were so called because their unbelievably cramped quarters was a single communal room in the bow just below the upper deck. The forward mast rudely pierced their already crowded hovel as it rose from the keel up through successive decks. Each wooden bunk alternately served two occupants. Places were exchanged every four hours as one watch was "relieved" and the other was summoned to the deck above. No hot-bed boardinghouse could have been more squalid. Cockroaches were one's constant companions at the onset of a whaling voyage. There was a small

compensation to the men in the bow; the first time the tryworks fires were blazing just above where the men slept, the entire roach population scrambled aft. Their "hoofbeats" could be readily heard. Relief could come if the ship was bound for Arctic or Antarctic whaling grounds—as the ship made its way into the higher latitudes, the cold would kill off the bugs completely.

Little more than 100 feet away in the stern of the vessel, the "old man" (this was an acceptable term for the captain *only* when speaking of him aboard the ship) resided in a modicum of ease—frequently with his wife and children. The good food eaten there and the other comforts afforded him could only be a wish and a dream for the others on the vessel. Yet there *were* bright moments to be savored in this isolated shipboard society.

The men were largely free from whatever confining strictures hobbled them at home. One's mates in the fo'c's'le might be black, Portuguese (from the islands off North Africa), Kanakas (from Hawaii and the South Pacific islands), Native Americans, convicts, street urchins, beachcombers or New England Yankees. One's worldview was quickly broadened on signing aboard a whaler. Slavery was still thriving in America in the eighteenth century and much of the nineteenth, and whaling offered black men a measure of personal and economic liberty. The Quakers of Nantucket were among the first to provide such opportunity.

Shipboard justice was often harshly meted out with the lash and the belaying pin. The shipping papers that were signed before setting sail did afford certain basic rights to the men, and the ship's officers could face charges if gross violations were brought to the attention of authorities in a port or when lodged at home in a court of law. Desertion rates could run from 20 to 30 percent, and it was frequently the way a sailor would remove himself from what he considered harsh conditions. In doing so, the sailor was technically in violation of his employment agreement and he forfeited his entire share in the voyage that may have accrued. Late in the cruise this could be a tidy sum. The officers whose own shares would thus increase might thus welcome the man's disappearance. Danger, too, was always present. It was quite an ordinary event to lose a shipmate to accident or disease. A doctor or any trained medical person did not exist at sea. One was at the mercy of the ship's captain and his medicine chest.

Everything a whaleman owned was tightly packed into his small sea chest, which was securely fastened to the deck of the fo'c's'le. Letters from home (as rare as they might be) would be safely bundled and read again and again. A letter addressed *to* home might also be prepared. If there was a chance encounter with a homeward-bound ship, letters were readily exchanged. Meeting another ship sometimes meant a "gam." A gam would be a very welcome meeting of the two ships. Clean clothes would come out of the sea chest and a hurried attempt at civilized grooming of one's person would be carried out. The two crews (who frequently knew each other) would get the opportunity to mingle, gossip, trade yarns, dance and sing. Treats and foodstuffs might be exchanged and provide a welcome break from their everyday chow. Yankee practicalities prevailed, however, and if whales were sighted, boats were readily lowered. Such hunting was frequently carried out as a joint venture, with the two ships cooperating, and sharing the proceeds of any kills.

Men frequently filled the countless idle hours at sea with scrimshaw, needlework, fancy ropework and other skills that they acquired. Though such projects could involve hundreds of hours to complete, a work in progress could be quite small and able to be stowed quickly away into one's sea chest. Fishing could be a way to pass the time as well. Turtles, flying fish and any number of other species could be caught and presented to the cook. The entire crew welcomed anything that could bring zest to the miserable daily fare. Shark steaks or roasted dolphin meat would be considered a feast.

The hardships of the voyage would be minimized when the boastful lads returned home. They would regale their lubberly friends with tales of giant monsters from the deep and dealings with cannibals, show off a bold tattoo, pass around souvenirs, and recount the charms of the beautiful island girls. If it was known that a man had actually wielded a harpoon and taken a whale, his prospects for business and marriage considerably brightened.

WHALEBONE CORSET BUSKS
Cold Spring Harbor Whaling Museum

The thin strips of baleen (called whalebone) that were found aplenty in the mouths of certain whales had some very desirable commercial properties. Baleen was tough, springy and flexible

The fashion in ladies' undergarments in the 1800s frequently emphasized a thin waist and prominent bust. Corsets made of cloth were sewn with narrow channels that could be fitted with whalebone. The delicate scrimshaw tracery on these two examples no doubt involved days (if not weeks) of a labor of love.

The initials MHS are inscribed at the center of the design to the right. The circular shapes are reminiscent of the compass rose that appears on navigation charts—or perhaps the compass card itself that is used to steer a course.

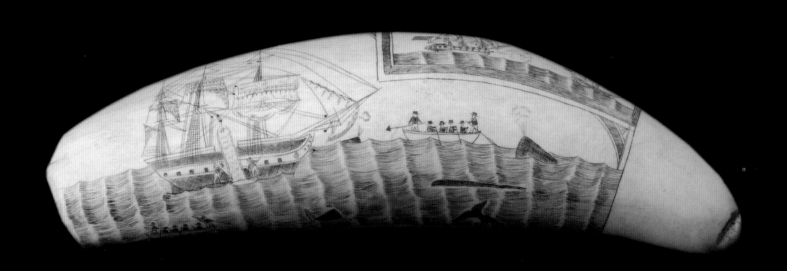

SPERM WHALE TOOTH, LIVELY WHALING GROUNDS
Cold Spring Harbor Whaling Museum

The scene depicted here shows a whaleship engaged in the process of cutting in. We can see that they have raised an enormous blanket piece of blubber from the whale alongside and are ready to board it. Two of the crew can be seen actually standing on the floating carcass with long cutting spades in hand.

At the same moment, if we consider this to be a snapshot of an instant in time, we see two whaleboats on the hunt with the smoothly rolling sea teeming with whales.

Ideally, the taking of whales was seen as a totally distinct operation from the cutting-in, with all hands required for the latter. But if there were whales to be had, surely the order to lower away would be heard.

WHALE TOOTH WITH SHIP AND EAGLE

Cold Spring Harbor Whaling Museum

The design is a finely detailed "stern-on" view of a "full rigged ship." The rendering of the patriotic "eagle" is humorously naïve. The very tip of the tooth is distressed but shows that it had been drilled. Undecorated teeth that have a drill hole raise the possibility that they were worn as a (quite heavy) neck decoration. A single sperm-whale tooth was considered a prized possession among many Pacific Islanders. Queen Elizabeth visited Fiji in 1953 and was presented with a tooth. It was the supreme gift to an honored visitor.

SPERM WHALE STAMP
Cold Spring Harbor Whaling Museum

This stamp is actually carved from the tooth of a sperm whale. Repeated use has left the carved area inky black. Every whaleman was taught to recognize whale types, even at a great distance, by their distinctive spouts. The true position of the sperm whale's single blowhole would be far forward—ahead of the curve of the snout. Unless a gale of wind was affecting it, the spouting spray would be directed ahead of the whale.

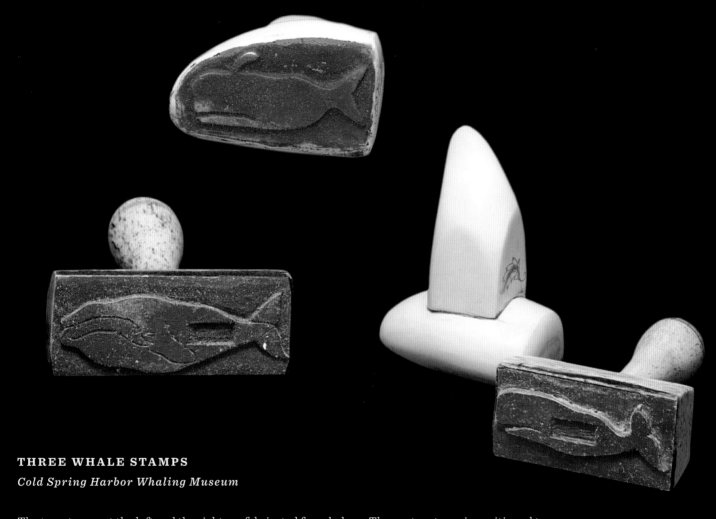

THREE WHALE STAMPS
Cold Spring Harbor Whaling Museum

The two stamps at the left and the right are fabricated from baleen. The center stamp is positioned to show that it's carved from sperm-whale tooth. A close look at the inky images shows the small mortised area that will remain clear when paper is stamped. Old logs and journals frequently have such stamped images. They graphically show the kind of whale captured. The number of barrels realized is written into the small mortised area.

The photographer regrets the contrary placement: the "right whale" is positioned on the left and the sperm whale is on the right.

FOUR WHALE STAMPS IN FRAME
Cold Spring Harbor Whaling Museum

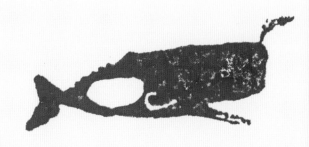

Stamps such as these were frequently carved from a scrap of sperm whale's tooth. The dense material was capable of recording the carver's fine detail. In addition to the official ship's log, journals were often kept by the men to record both hunting successes and "the ones that got away."

The four whale carvings shown here in a museum mounted frame would have been used to record successful catches. The record keeper would select from the four species depicted here, ink the surface and print an impression on the page. There is an oval void in the body of each whale, to record the number of barrels of oil extracted from each kill.

The shape of the whale's body was an immediate identifier to the men as was the distinctive shape of the spout. Looking at the images in the frame (from top to bottom) we have a sperm whale, humpback, bowhead or right whale. The fourth is somewhat of a mystery. It seems to be a fin whale, a species that was not hunted from boats because of its incredible speed. It was taken in later days with the advent of steam vessels.

ONE-HAND GAME OF SKILL

Sag Harbor Whaling Museum

The whalebone handle is held vertically with the small nib at the top. The spiky ivory ball hangs freely the full length of the cord. By swinging the ball in an arc and giving a last-second jiggle, one attempts to have the orb perform a half somersault and seat its large circular opening on the nib.

    The carved spikes can freely rattle around—each in their individual hole and merely add movement and wonder—as in "I wonder how the carver managed that!" The overall shape echoes a deadly battle flail from medieval times.

WHALEBONE—PECKING-BIRDS TOY

Sag Harbor Whaling Museum

The handle at the left holds the toy. The knob is allowed to hang as a counterweight to the articulated birds. By jiggling the weight the birds seem to frantically peck the ground for corn or feed.

HORSE AND CART WITH RED HARNESS
Sag Harbor Whaling Museum

This is shaped from the bone of a whale rather than carved from its ivory. The speckled grain is apparent. It has precisely turned wheels of two sizes and nicely curved shafts on the cart.

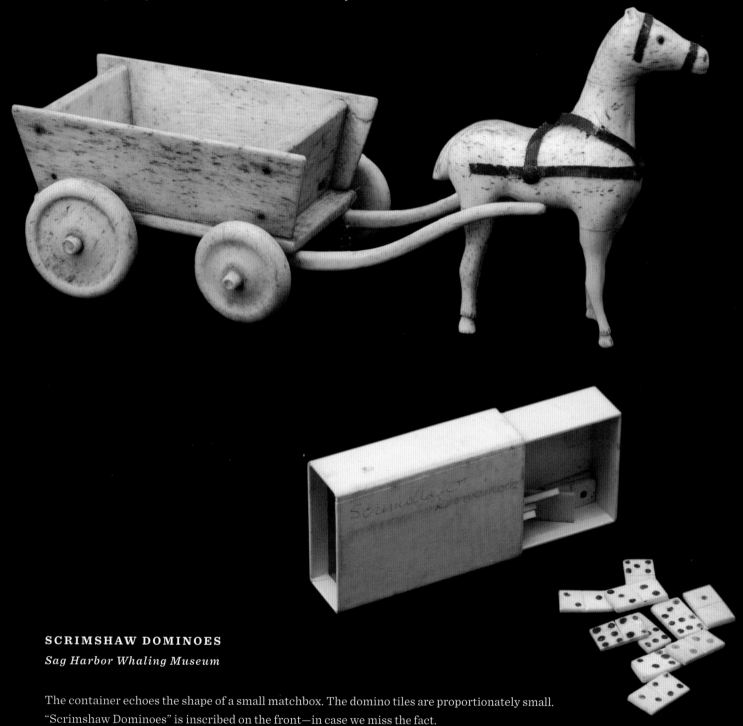

SCRIMSHAW DOMINOES
Sag Harbor Whaling Museum

The container echoes the shape of a small matchbox. The domino tiles are proportionately small. "Scrimshaw Dominoes" is inscribed on the front—in case we miss the fact.

IVORY RING WITH WHALING SCENE

Sag Harbor Whaling Museum

The foreground shows men in a whaleboat pulling at the oars. The grain of the ivory is showing its age.

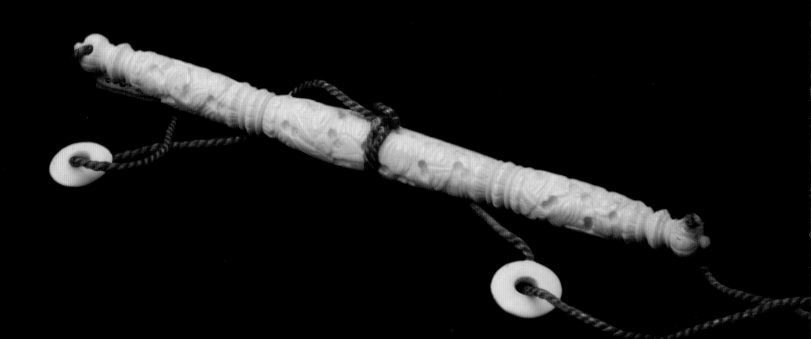

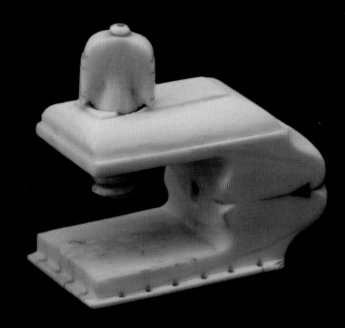

CARVED IVORY CLAMP
Sag Harbor Whaling Museum

The function here is similar to that of a C-clamp. The artist is showing off his skills by carving very precise male and female threads. This probably would have been an attachment for a swift—the device used by knitters and weavers for handling yarn.

MINIATURE DUCK OR GOOSE
Sag Harbor Whaling Museum

The head and body appear to be separate pieces of bone (rather than ivory) fitted together.

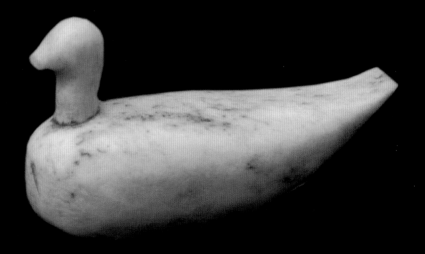

IVORY ELEPHANT, TWO VIEWS
Sag Harbor Whaling Museum

The carver worked and polished a mere scrap of whale ivory to make this whimsical little fellow. The anatomical scale is fanciful rather than literal. He's missing a bit of his own "ivory"—the right tusk is broken off.

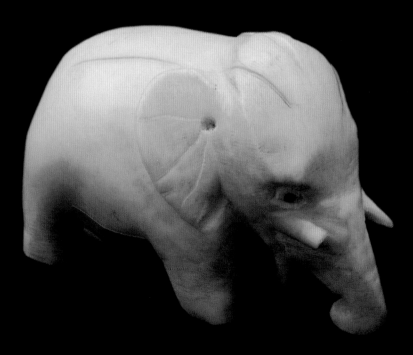

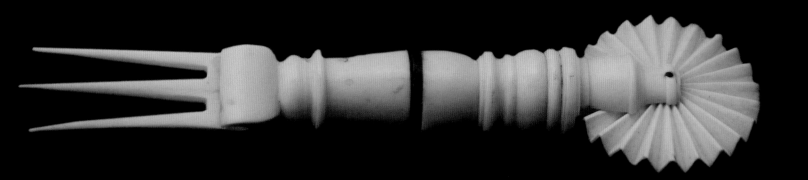

JAGGING WHEEL (PIE CRIMPER) WITH THREE TINES
Sag Harbor Whaling Museum

The toolmaker knows well how the cook will put this to use. The wheel at one end will put a zigzag design into the dough. The final touch before putting the pie in the oven is often pricking holes in the dough of the upper crust to allow steam to escape.

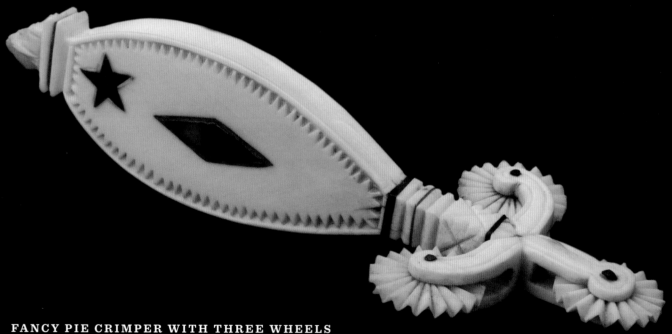

FANCY PIE CRIMPER WITH THREE WHEELS
Sag Harbor Whaling Museum

As already noted, these items represent the high art of the whale-tooth carver. Each of the three wheels is precisely mounted on a decorative clevis. The inlaid star and diamond shapes are surrounded by an oval of little "saw teeth" that subtly illustrate how the tool will leave its mark on the pie dough. Inlay materials that are frequently seen are wood, silver, stone, tortoiseshell, mother of pearl and abalone shell.

OIL CASK AND TRYPOT
Nantucket Whaling Museum

The trypot above is of a smaller capacity. The smallest "standard" size was about 140 gallons. When this pot was twinned with another and the two flat sides abutted, the notches in the opposing rims would line up. A trough of sheet metal connecting the two pots would allow liquids and solid pieces to be moved from one pot to the other without a drop spilling into the firebox below.

The cask that is shown is made from oak staves and riveted iron hoops. It would have been lying snugly (on its side) deep in the hold of the ship. The fill hole that we see (the bung) would be positioned at the top. A system of pipes and hoses of leather or canvas would direct the flow, and then the bung would be plugged shut. The contents of two of the iron kettles shown would just about fill this cask. Care was taken (especially in hot latitudes) to spray the filled oak casks with water. This was to keep the wood fibers plump and leakproof.

WOODEN HOOPS AND STRAIGHT HEAD STOCK
New Bedford Whaling Museum

The cooper possessed the skill to take these simple materials and make containers that held tight in storage and eventually could be hoisted, rolled, steeved, warehoused and otherwise "manhandled" without spilling a precious drop.

The flat "heads" had to be made up of several planks that joined together perfectly. Metal hoops would seem a more reliable material for hooping the cask, but the cooper was asked to make barrels for all kinds of storage. Pine staves were frequently carried aboard by the thousands for use in dry, nonoily storage containers.

WOODEN OIL-BARREL GAUGE
Martha's Vineyard Museum

The value of whale oil at the marketplace was reckoned on its volume rather than its weight. Handmade barrels that varied from the norm were common. This wooden device is calibrated in inches and would help to establish the number of gallons that a container held.

SMALL BARRELS AND COOPER'S LEVER
New Bedford Whaling Museum

As the largest casks began to fill the hold, space became more precious. Smaller casks and barrels were fashioned to make use of the irregular-shaped areas around the large containers, between ship timbers and other odd niches. One small cask was called a "ryer." It's thought that the name comes from "rider," which is one of the structural timbers coming up from the keel.

Certain oils would be given their own container. Spermaceti, blackfish oil, sea-elephant oil, and porpoise-jaw oil might be collected in smaller amounts, yet commanded good prices at market.

The tool shown here is a simple lever that the cooper could use to flex the shape of a single stave as a barrel was being assembled.

COOPER'S SHAVING HORSE
New Bedford Whaling Museum

This is a simple wood clamp. The worker puts a board into the horse's "mouth" (it is shown "closed" here), and foot pressure on the treadle will hold the board firmly while he or a coworker is able to use a two-handed tool like a drawknife or spokeshave to taper or shape the piece.

A variation of this tool was used for turning planks of wood into tapered shingles. The tongue-twister lyric in the child's song is "Shave a cedar shingle thin."

COOPER'S MALLET
Cold Spring Harbor Whaling Museum

The cooper was a vital hand on a whaleship. His quarters were aft with the other elite of the crew. He was allotted ample room for his work-space and material storage. His generous "lay," or compensation agreement, indicated his importance to the overall success of the voyage. It was expected that his assembly of wooden containers for newly "tried out" oil and maintenance of full, stowed casks would be flawless. This narrow wooden tool would tap the narrow hoops that girded the cask snugly in place.

BARRELS WITH METAL HOOPS
Whaleship **Charles W. Morgan**
Mystic Seaport

The men would size up a whale (even in pursuit) as, for instance, an "80-barrel bull" or "60-barrel cow." If they had hunting success, there would be an immediate need for scores of containers such as seen here to stow down the oil.

An 80-barrel bull did not necessitate the making of 80 barrels. A "barrel" was a standard unit of measurement equal to 30.5 gallons. Some casks could hold ten times that amount. The point is, the cooper was always very busy when whales were being taken.

SHOOKS AND HEADS
Whaleship **Charles W. Morgan**
Mystic Seaport

To save space as they set out on a voyage, thousands of preworked parts would be bundled together. The bundle to the left might be described as a "barrel full of barrel parts"—a shook. It's a little less than 3 feet in diameter at the fattest part.

To the far left is a partially made-up "head" that will close both ends. The simple two-layer lamination is shown. One can see that it is to be a *huge* vessel. The metal hoops for binding it all together are underneath.

OAK BARREL STAVES
Whaleship **Charles W. Morgan**
Mystic Seaport

The staves have been given a bend before being bundled for the voyage. The cooper will use simple tools and sharp skills to fit everything together snugly.

The cooper had great status on a whaleship. If all of the ship's officers, including the captain, had "lowered" in pursuit of whales, the cooper was next in the chain of command. He was designated "shipkeeper" and made the necessary decisions and maneuvers until the boats were safely back in their davits.

SHIPMATE 450 COOKING STOVE
Whaleship Charles W. Morgan
Mystic Seaport

The firebox is fed through the small door
at the left with the "450" on it. Coal, wood
or even whale scrap could provide the heat.
The handle (the angled metal tool on the
stove surface) can be inserted in the little
hole below that door to rattle the cinders
and ashes through a grate into the collector
at the very bottom. The large door at the
right with the SHIPMATE lettering is the oven.

The iron "fence" around the cooking
surface is called the fiddle. Its purpose it to
keep cooking pots from sliding away when the
seas are up. Another feature shown here is the
adjustment mechanism to corral the big pots
and pans more snugly.

The white wall just to the rear of the
cooking surface is actually a door that swings
out and up. Prepared food can be dispensed
from there without disturbing the cook in his
tiny galley.

CAPTAIN'S PANTRY
Whaleship Charles W. Morgan
Mystic Seaport

The only natural light and ventilation here is the small porthole in the center. The captain, the steward or
perhaps the captain's spouse had access to provisions that the foremast hands could only dream of.

Boring, spartan or downright disgusting meals were all too often the crew's fare. Anything interesting
that they could catch on a hook or spear with a harpoon would be brought to the cook and shared by all.
Dolphin, seals, turtles and birds could sometimes be gotten while they were under way. If they put in at an
island (frequently in pursuit of freshwater and firewood), they had a keen eye for fruits, vegetables, wild
pigs and anything else that could be used.

Certain captains were known to be quite social. This would, of course, be with other ship's officers,
merchants, agents and others that they perceived as "quality" folk. The captain's larder was likely to have
fine wines, spirits, tobacco, nuts, fruits and other choice provisions.

CAPTAIN'S DINING TABLE

Whaleship Charles W. Morgan
Mystic Seaport

No, the hole in the mahogany is not for the salad bowl. In fact, the semblance of roominess is deceiving when you realize that the mizzenmast will once again fill that space. All the masts have been pulled from the *Morgan* until the restorations are completed. The fiddle is the raised rim around the edge of the table. It and the longitudinal strips are to keep food and utensils from sliding away in rough seas.

Many captains preferred to dine alone. Others welcomed the company of their officers and other worthies.

CAPTAIN'S GIMBALED BED

Whaleship Charles W. Morgan
Mystic Seaport

The vertical white post in the foreground has a bearing, which is attached to the footboard of the bed. There is a second bearing holding the headboard at the other end. As the ship rolls from side to side, this gimbaled arrangement acts to keep the bed (and the sleeper) on the level.

The captain (and his wife, if she's on the voyage) were the only ones afforded such comfort on the *Morgan.*

SINK AND WASHSTAND IN CAPTAIN'S SLEEPING CHAMBER

Whaleship Charles W. Morgan

Mystic Seaport

No shower or porcelain tub was in evidence aboard the *Morgan,* but here, at least, we have a porcelain sink. The upper hole would cradle a washbasin for shaving and bathing.

REAR BULKHEAD (WALL) IN CAPTAIN'S SITTING ROOM

Whaleship Charles W. Morgan

Mystic Seaport

The sitting room has also been known as the salon or the saloon. A large skylight above (not shown) allows one to peer into this less private area of the captain's quarters from the main deck, just above. Several of its glass panels can be opened for ventilation. It provides a good measure of light for the captain's comfort. The two portholes shown here can be opened inward for ventilation. They also provide a bit of light above the bookshelves and storage drawers.

It's quite civilized here. A built-in settee is upholstered in red plush fabric. There is a crisp, finished look to the carpentry. Every bit of space is creatively used for shelving, drawers, cupboards and cabinets. The captain of a whaleship frequently had his wife and family travel with him. On land they could live very well. Every attempt seems to have been made here on the *Morgan* to treat the captain as a man of privilege, entitled to a fine "quality of life."

CAPTAIN'S SALON, DETAIL
Whaleship Charles W. Morgan
Mystic Seaport

The red plush settee has its back to the stern of the vessel. The huge rudder is just a few feet away. The door to the right with the louvered panel leads to a companionway with steps to the main deck. This arrangement allows the captain to be at the helm in seconds.

COMMODE (HEAD) IN CAPTAIN'S QUARTERS
Whaleship Charles W. Morgan
Mystic Seaport

This is not really a two-holer. It might be described as a combination commode and garbage disposal unit. The tiny space is located just aft of the sleeping chamber on the starboard side. There is very little room overhead. As you can see, cupboards are placed wherever space allows.

OUTHOUSE (HEAD) ON THE PORT BOW
Upper Deck, Whaleship Charles W. Morgan
Mystic Seaport

The door has been removed for paint scraping before repainting. The only other "moving part" of this sanitary device seems to be the hinged cover of the "seat of ease." It's positioned directly over the water. It was the only such facility for all of the foremast crew.

On many whaleships, urine was collected for laundry use. The ship itself as well as the men's work clothes would be conscientiously cleaned following the filth of the cutting-in and trying-out. Vinegar was liberally used for cleaning and degreasing the decks and other parts of the ship. The urine was used for soaking the grime out of the men's clothing. They would be thoroughly rinsed in seawater—as freshwater was too precious. A rainsquall would be a welcome rinse at the end of laundry day to restore softness to their garments.

LIGHT-GATHERING PRISMS IN FIRST OFFICER'S QUARTERS

Whaleship Charles W. Morgan

Mystic Seaport

We're looking at the "overhead" (ceiling) in the first mate's small living quarters. There are no windows (portholes) or any other source of natural light, so two polished glass prisms have been fitted into the weather deck above. In jest it might be called a passive solar system. In sunny daylight hours cheerful little glimmers might aid in reading a chart or making a log entry. On a "cloudy bright" day the devices would help to eliminate the dark-as-a-dungeon ambiance that was experienced elsewhere belowdecks.

FIRST OFFICER'S CABIN
Whaleship Charles W. Morgan
Mystic Seaport

This is very compact space, but it represents the second-best accommodations that the *Morgan* has to offer. It is but a few steps away from the captain's much more spacious quarters and is provided with a raised bunk with storage space below it. There is a chart table and gimbaled oil lamp, which allows him to keep up his daily navigation and log duties. The bulkhead (wall) that slopes inward toward his bunk shows the curvature of the hull. The main deck is just a few feet above his head.

Evidence of the fact that the first mate's quarters represented an inner sanctum quite off-limits to the crew billeted at the far end of the ship is the fact that the fierce "boarding knife" was often stowed under his bunk for ultrasafekeeping when whales were not being butchered.

BRASS SPEAKING TRUMPET

Martha's Vineyard Museum

Much has been written about the secrecy that surrounded whaling. However, ships that were far from home *would* share certain basic information when hailed by a passing ship. Short, crisp queries would demand over the noise of wind and waves: "What vessel are you?"; "From which port?"; "How much oil?" This brass "horn," or trumpet, was a slight improvement over simply cupping one's hands at the mouth. It also might have been put to the ear as a "receiver."

Crews knew that by contributing and collecting such information on this simple grapevine at sea that the news of their "most recent sighting" would be published in a trade newspaper in New Bedford. Family, investors, shipowners and townsfolk were greedy for such news.

The *Whalemen's Shipping List and Merchants' Transcript* was published weekly from 1843 until 1914. Archival copies stand as a valuable record of U.S. whaling.

SEA CAPTAIN'S LAP DESK

Private Collection
of Ryan M. Cooper
YARMOUTHPORT, MASSACHUSETTS

There is faint writing on the inlaid walrus-ivory plaque at the top of the piece that indicates that it was both made and owned by Captain Frederick H. Smith. He is very well known for his fine scrimshaw work. He made this item while on an 1876 voyage on the *Ohio*.

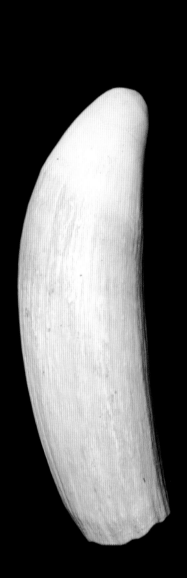

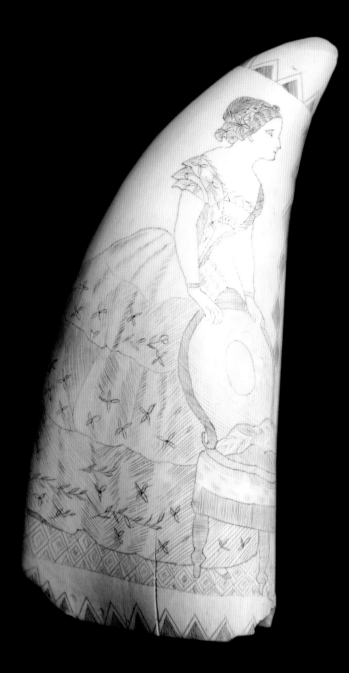

SPERM WHALE TOOTH

Nantucket Whaling Museum

This is a sperm whale tooth that doesn't seem to have been worked or polished. The smooth white tip may have been the only part that protruded from the whale's gum line. Whale ivory is very dense and can have a heavy feel in the hand.

SCRIMSHAWED TOOTH

Nantucket Whaling Museum

This sperm whale's tooth had been polished before the images of a fashionable young lady and uphol-stered chair were added. Subsequently, the design was polychromed—colored pigments were added.

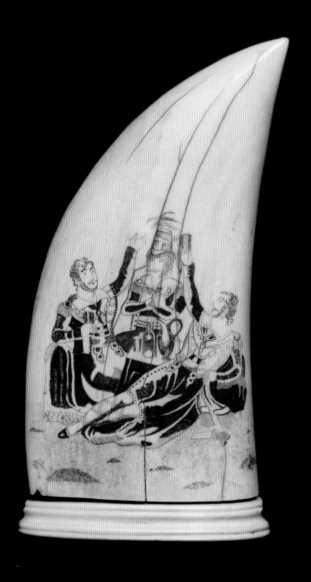

TWO ILLUSTRATED SPERM-WHALE TEETH

Nantucket Whaling Museum

These teeth have been smoothed and highly polished. They have been decorated in a distinctive style by a
skilled illustrator. The thick fields of black ink give the images the contrasty look of a woodcut.

FIVE DECORATED SPERM-WHALE TEETH, TWO VIEWS

Nantucket Whaling Museum

The teeth that tend to curve to the right have other common traits. Each has a lower border, a garland wrapping around the tip and a cameo of a female figure.

The reverse of each tooth, shown below, has either a maritime drawing or a nature scene. The maritime scenes are drawn to be seen in the horizontal.

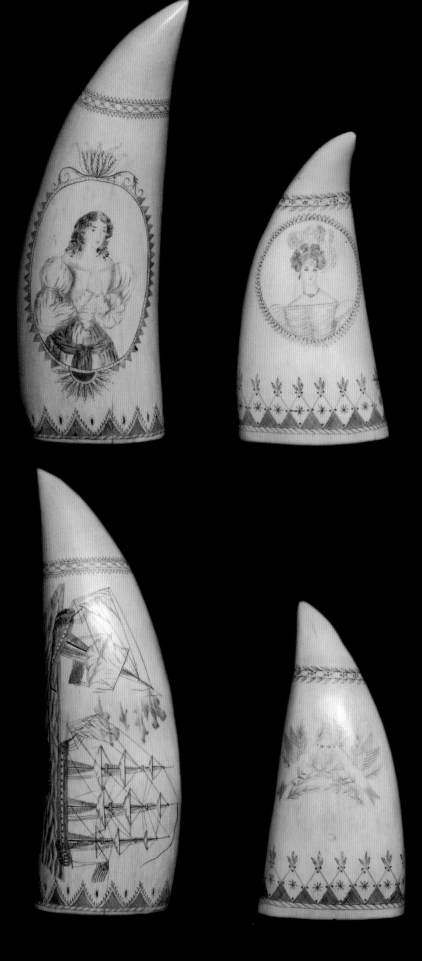

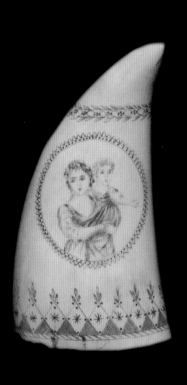

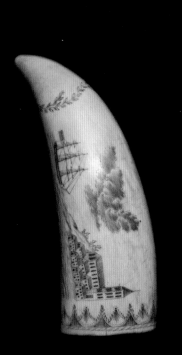

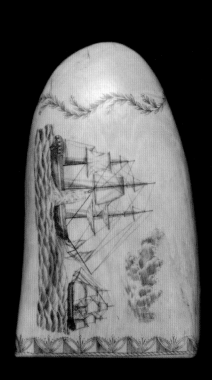

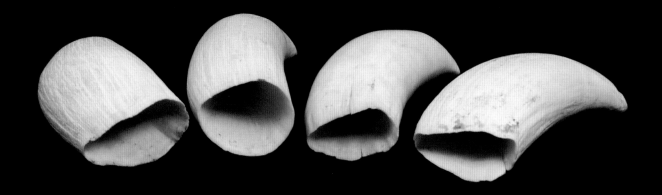

SCRIMSHAW TECHNIQUE

Nantucket Whaling Museum

When scrimshaw became popular in the early 1800s, a sperm-whale tooth became a prized possession of a whaleman. As he was planning his design he would begin to sand and polish the rough, raw tooth. He might borrow a rasp or file from the carpenter or cooper for the initial smoothing. A shark's skin would work as a medium abrasive. Rottenstone, pumice and wood ash could be used for final polishing. Having a shipmate such as a cabin boy (who might still have soft hands) repeatedly rub it was also a possibility.

The tooth with the paper overlay shows how a design could be clipped from a magazine as a template. Needle pricks would be used as guides. The idea was to "connect-the-dots" with a line that covered these points, giving the illusion of a freehand drawing. The vast amount of scrimshaw that survives today shows a range of skills from awkwardness and naïveté to absolute artistry and virtuosity.

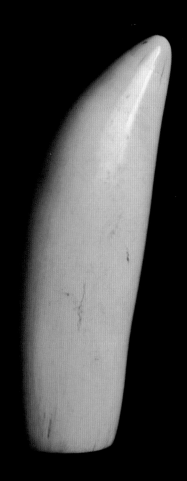 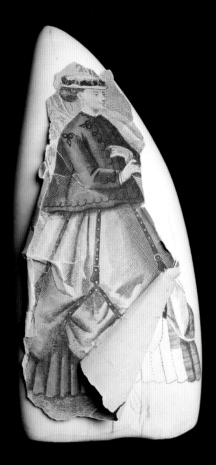

SPERM-WHALE TOOTH IN WOODEN DISPLAY TRAY, TWO VIEWS
Nantucket Whaling Museum

The female figure on one side is handling a length of ribbon, perhaps for her hair. Both sides of the tooth have delicately rendered, oversized botanical drawings.

The second view shows a bird in the branches above an unusual three-story house with smoke wafting from each of the chimneys. The two sides of the house show a total of fifteen windows.

The graphic design and wooden tray suggest an Asian influence.

IVORY POCKET WATCH DISPLAY STAND

Nantucket Whaling Museum

This delicate piece is likely made up of whale or walrus ivory—or a combination of the two. Much of the inlay material is tortoiseshell. It would mount on a shelf, mantel or side table. The watch was easily accessible for frequent winding.

THREE DECORATED TEETH
ON A WOODEN BASE
Nantucket Whaling Museum

The scrimshander has worked carefully to render the three female costumes here in great detail. The faces of each of the three figures may have been specially polished or had white pigment applied. They remain "fair" even though most neutral areas of the background have yellowed with age. The figure on the right is playing cards.

THREE INLAID WHALE-IVORY CUPS
Martha's Vineyard Museum

The upper part of each cup is carved from sperm-whale tooth and given the saw-toothed edge. The borders, birds, vines, flowers and fruit all seem to be created with inlaid baleen, mother of pearl and other shells such as abalone. It appears that no (or little) ink was used to create the design. The cup on the left shows where thin strips have come away.

SPERM WHALE CANDLE WITH FANCY GLASS REFLECTOR
Private Collector

The crisp, clear light from a spermaceti candle was a welcome innovation in home lighting. The tallow candles that they replaced (rendered from beef or pig fat) were greasy, sooty, smelly and cast an inferior yellow light.

ENGRAVING PLATE FOR NANTUCKET BANKNOTES

Phoenix Bank

Nantucket Whaling Museum

This hand-engraved copper plate (the image on the right has been reversed and shown in monochrome for legibility) would reproduce banknotes in TEN, TWENTY, THIRTY and FORTY dollar denominations. The printed sheets would be trimmed at the thin double line that separates each bill.

The worldwide financial might enjoyed by the tiny island is on display here. The piece of paper printed from this plate, once numbered and put into circulation, would be accepted in exchange for goods, services and other considerations with the confidence that the Phoenix Bank of Nantucket would pay the face value to the bearer—in cash.

The engraver has employed a wide variety of graphic elements to foil counterfeiters. We see the "thick and thin" swirls of Spenserian script, block lettering, scrolls, wreaths, ships and spouting whales. The plate has been defaced with random scratches. This may have been done purposely to show that any further printing is void and nonnegotiable.

Chapter Ten

LIFE ASHORE

Old Nantucket is but a pinpoint of an island. Its position 26 miles from nearby Cape Cod leaves her in a position where she must fend for herself. The early white settlers were mostly pious people, but their religious views ran counter to the Congregationalist, or Puritan, establishment on the mainland. A census in the late 1600s showed that among the few families living on Nantucket there were Baptists, Presbyterians and an odd sect that had sprung up in England a few decades earlier, the Religious Society of Friends—or Quakers.

The Friends, as they called each other, believed in the worship of God without the necessity of a preacher or other clergy; they had no liturgy or sacraments. They were inspired by the "inner light" of the Holy Spirit and held that every man had that light within him. In secular matters they refused to take oaths, use honorific titles or forms of address of any kind including Sir, Lord or Your Excellency. They disdained violence against any man no matter what the cause. They refused to join an army or mili-

tia. Their plain and unadorned dress matched their simple manner of address: "thee," "thy" and "thou." Kindness and humility was woven into their way of life. Needless to say, they so rankled the Puritans of the Massachusetts colony that it was decreed that the mere presence of Quakers in a village should result in "whipping-out." A second "offense" could mean hanging. Still, the Quakers of that era were a feisty lot.

The Society of Friends flourished on Nantucket, and their skill at killing the sperm whale gave rise to a vast and prosperous industrial empire. In time, the Nantucket "Meeting of Worship" would become a "Meeting of Commerce." The "Quaker paradox" was evident for some one hundred years with several confounding variations.

Whaling was an important industry for the American colonies just at the time that they were wrestling themselves free from the English monarchy and other European influence. Since England was the prime market for Nantucket whale oil, both sides demanded of the little island: Are you Patriot, or are you Loyalist, a Tory?

Nantucket skillfully hedged the question. They truly had a vein of Patriot loyalties. The Crown sensed this and would plunder her supplies, blockade her ports, cause her ships to rot at their moorings, and harass what ships she found on the high seas. In turn, Nantucket's citizens were rebuked by the colonials as British sympathizers and accused of using the Quaker way of nonviolence to cowardly refuse to send men to support General Washington's army. Neither side could be sure of Nantucket's leanings. Nantucket justly pleaded "neutrality," which neither side was readily willing to grant. In hindsight, it can be seen that their sentiments were clearly "Nantucket First."

No one played the Quaker paradox more skillfully than William Rotch (pronounced *Roach*). He was perhaps the prototypical international business mogul. He kept his Nantucket and Quaker loyalties while dealing cleverly (and quite honorably) with England, France and our emerging American republic. He adroitly steered his vast fleet of ships among friendly nations and hostile nations. Whoever said "The business of America *is* business" might well have said it of William Rotch and his family that followed. With intuition, diplomacy, persuasion, courage and pure Yankee moxie, Rotch

personally lobbied the likes of Washington, Jefferson, Monroe, Franklin, George III, Louis XVI, Talleyrand, and William Pitt. One of his ships, the *Dartmouth*, was central to the tax protest known as the Boston Tea Party. When his ships were impeded by war from leaving from Nantucket, he temporarily established his headquarters in the Falkland Islands! His whaleships and merchant ships were known and respected in virtually every port on Earth.

The whaling trade invigorated the economic life of the coastal towns. The commodities harvested, whale oil and baleen, were readily snapped up to satisfy the myriad requirements of the burgeoning industrial revolution. Streetlights in all the major cities of the world burned whale oil. Sophisticated machinery in textile mills ran smoothly thanks to the unmatched lubricity of spermaceti oil. America wished to say goodbye to its frontier past, and smoky tallow candles for home lighting lost favor to the bright and smokeless spermaceti variety. At one point there were more than a score of spermaceti candle factories on tiny Nantucket.

The tons of baleen harvested from the upper jaw of a single right or humpback whale would find their way into dozens of consumer goods. Baleen was the light, strong and flexible material that gave shape to umbrellas, hoop skirts and other fashionable undergarments. Its reliable springiness was used extensively in machine parts until eclipsed by newly developed and patented spring steel. Nantucket ships continued to hunt mainly the sperm whale, which had no baleen, but other whalers frequently returned with a cargo quite evenly divided between oil and "bone," as the baleen was commercially known.

Shipbuilders and whaleboat builders thrived, as did chandlers, ropeworks, block-makers, sailmakers, insurers, banks, coopers, blacksmiths, masons, caulkers, grogshops, rooming houses and land sharks, the wily employment agents that the shipowners came to rely upon to fill out their crews with gullible, inexperienced young men. The outbound vessels enriched the economy, as did those that successfully returned.

As the enterprise prospered, with Nantucket as its center, Rotch and his fellow islanders (with names like Starbuck, Coffin, Macy, Gardener, Hussey and Russell) realized that having an addi-tional base of operation on the mainland would be an advantage. A little settlement on the Acushnet River was selected. The whaling town of New Bedford would blossom on the site. It offered a sheltered location, deep harbor, unlimited potential for wharf space, warehouses, shipbuilding and all the other requirements for both outfitting ships for hunting and then receiving their cargoes on return. New Bedford grew into one of the wealthiest cities in the United States. It saw the golden age of whaling as well as its sunset.

Lat. 31..59..0 S. . SPERM .WHALING. . Long. 159..0..0 E.-

SPERM WHALING SCENE SHOWING LORD HOWE ISLAND, SCRIMSHAW ON PANBONE

Lat. 31-59-0 S., Long. 159-0-0 E

Nantucket Whaling Museum

The whaler who recorded this interesting scene was far from home. We now know from the coordinates that he inscribed that he was at Lord Howe Island. This is a beautiful, tiny speck of an island in the vast sea between Australia and New Zealand. (It's part of Australia.) The productive whaling grounds were a few hours' sail from the island itself, but ships would position themselves in the protected "lee" of the island to process their caught whales.

The islands were uninhabited during the early days of whaling. Initially, three men settled there to plant foods that could be sold to the many visiting ships. A small settlement soon followed. Descendants of those "founding fathers" inhabit the island today. The "international" popularity of the whaling site can be imagined from the "flags of nations" that decorate the top of the piece.

The shape of the island's distinctive mountains was quite faithfully recorded. Today it's known to expert surfers for the large waves that break against its dangerous coast. It is also a peaceful spot to study distinctive bird, plant and marine life.

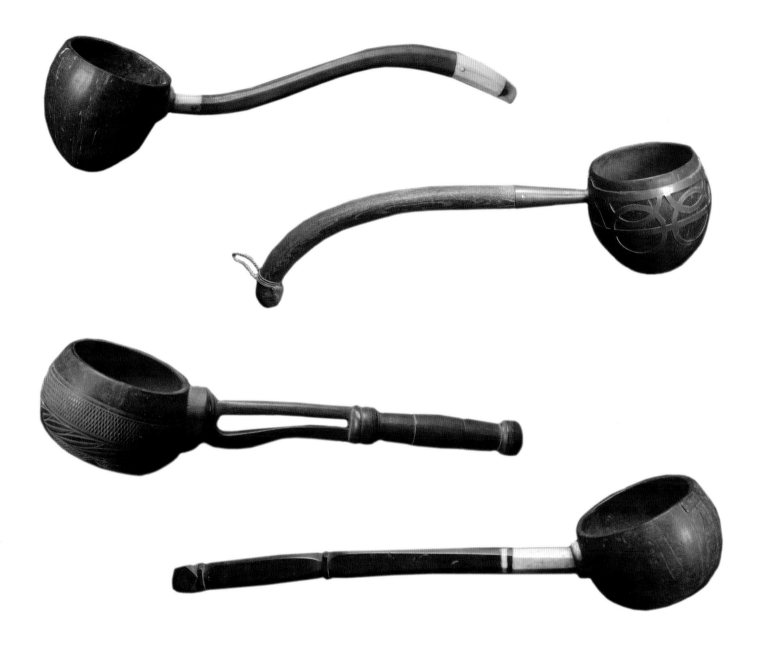

FOUR DIPPERS WITH COCONUT-SHELL BOWLS

Cold Spring Harbor Whaling Museum

Fresh water for the crew was kept in a cask (butt) that had been "scuttled"—one end was removed. Dippers such as those shown here might well have hung next to the "scuttlebutt" for communal use. They were also brought home as souvenirs of voyages to the tropics. The fanciful designs may have been the work of the sailors themselves or Polynesian craftsmen.

The examples here show the coconut shell bowl, wooden handles, metal filigree, delicate island carving, and bone, ivory and mineral turnings. The last example shows a tiny brass repair to the lip of the bowl.

NECK ORNAMENT, LEI NEHI PALAOA

Kauai Cultural Museum

KAUAI, HAWAII

When one sees the word "lei" one thinks of an ornamental circle
of fragrant flowers. Here, "Lei Nehi Palaoa" means a necklace that is
made up of a carved sperm whale's tooth as a pendant from a thick bundle of braided human hair. It was
worn by tribal chieftains. One wonders if the original owners of the hair gave it up voluntarily.

SCRIMSHAW ON PANBONE, *THE SAILOR'S RETURN*

Nantucket Whaling Museum

Panbone polishes up well and offers a reasonably flat surface for the artist to work. The tapers and
curves on a tooth offer more challenges. The decorative border inscribed here frames the "land and
sea" division nicely.

   The most widely accepted name for the artist who works in this uniquely American art form is
"scrimshander." Martha Lawrence, in her book *Scrimshaw: The Whaler's Legacy,* has found several
different ways that the men described the activity. The artist was sometimes known as a scrimshawer.
The activity has been described as scrimshonting, scrimshoning, scrimshanting and scrimshorning.

   There was a wide gulf between the written word and the spoken word. "Sperm" might be spelled
"spirm" or "sparm." Similarly, the stern of the vessel might be written (or spoken) "starn."

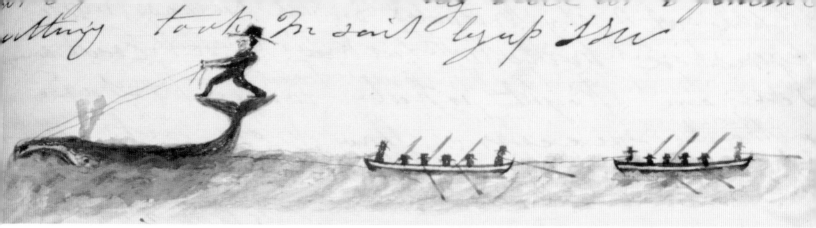

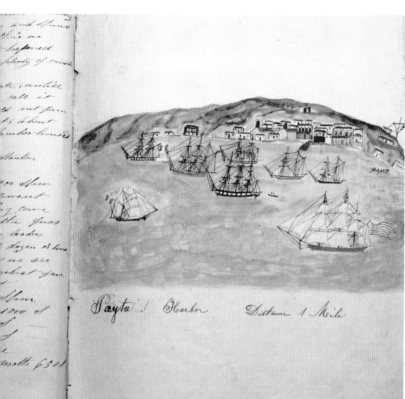

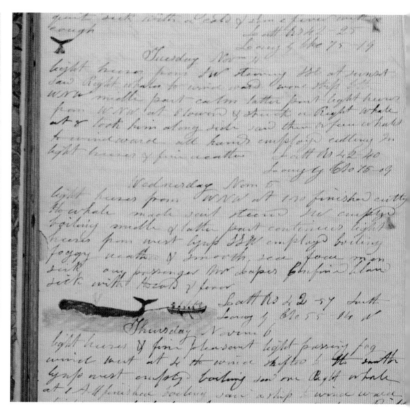

JOURNAL ENTRIES FROM THE WHALESHIP *SUSAN*

Cruise of 1841–1846

Capt. Reuben Russell, Keeper

Captain Reuben Russell was a successful Nantucket whaler who had additional talents. He shows a skilled hand as an illustrator and he had a sense of humor. The entries shown here are from the journal he kept during the four-and-a-half-year cruise on the *Susan*.

One ink sketch with watercolor flourishes is a self-parody showing him standing atop the flukes of a right whale holding reins as if he's driving a team. (It was often noted that Quaker whalers dressed like farmers.) The whale is obviously doomed. Russell has given a pink wash to the spout to indicate that the whale has been lanced. The bloody display of "fire in the chimney" signals that the end is near.

One of the entries shows ships clustered in the harbor at one of their "ports of call." Elsewhere there is a depiction of the whaling grounds among the Galápagos Islands.

R.H. MACY BURIAL SITE

Woodlawn Cemetery

BRONX, NEW YORK

Macy's is the giant department store enterprise with the prominent red star emblazoned on their packaging. The company (formerly known as R. H. Macy & Company) can trace its corporate lineage directly back to the whaling industry.

Macy is a storied name among early Nantucket Quakers. The family was involved in every aspect of whaling. One of their number was Rowland Hussey Macy (1822–1877). The small dry-goods store that he began in 1858 has grown into the giant marketer that we know today.

R.H. undertook a whaling voyage at the age of fifteen. He returned from that adventure with a *red star* tattooed on his hand.

INUIT CARVED WHALEBONE FIGURE

Bill Cannon Collection

BREWSTER, MASSACHUSETTS

The 4-inch figure in a hooded parka, or anorak, was deftly carved (probably in the early twentieth century) from an ancient piece of whalebone. It, no doubt, lay exposed to the elements for centuries before being worked by the carver. As bone that forms the ribs, vertebrae and other structures dries out and ages, it shows its true nature, which is lightweight, porous and honeycombed. The artist has given his little figure "body language" that is bold and confident.

ESQUIMAUX SUN GOGGLES, TWO VIEWS
Martha's Vineyard Museum

This item might have been more than a sailor's souvenir from a voyage to an exotic land. It reminds us that New England whalers found themselves working and living in close contact with cultures far different from their own—often for months at a time. In the subpolar regions of the Pacific it was sometimes arranged that a ship would "lay up" for the frigid season and the crew would live and work among the native population. Whaling activity could be suspended and hunting for seal, walrus and other sources of oil, fur and ivory could be pursued.

These goggles have no glass or lenses but are ingeniously carved from a single piece of wood. Thin slits mask off the glare from a blinding sun on the ice and snow. A hole at each side would have held a loop of cord or rawhide to keep them in place.

Written accounts frequently read "Esquimaux" as opposed to our more frequent "Eskimo."

DECORATED POUCH WITH DRAWSTRING
Martha's Vineyard Museum

This cloth bag, decorated with stitchery, is obviously a keepsake from a voyage to the north.

SPERM-WHALE TOOTH WITH EROTIC SCENE AND POEM, TWO VIEWS
Nantucket Whaling Museum

The left-hand view shows the couple in an embrace with the words of the woman's poem above and below.

The scene on the reverse side shows a fully clothed woman who is pointing to the ring position on the third finger of her left hand.

An easy yielding maid,
By trusting is undone;
Our sex is oft betray'd,
By granting love too soon.
If you desire to gain me,
Your suffering to redress;
She said. O kiss me longer,
And longer yet, and longer,
Before you shall possess.

But his kiss was so sweet, and so closely he prest,
That I languished and pin'd till I granted the rest.

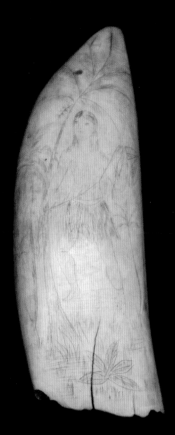
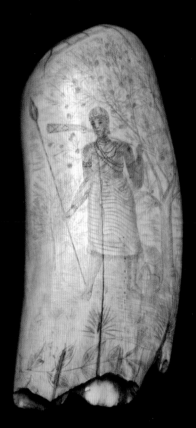
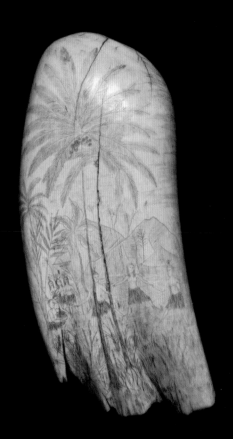

SPERM-WHALE TEETH DEPICTING SOUTH SEA IMAGES
Nantucket Whaling Museum

The cracks and discoloration on these teeth probably reflect a long shelf life. They provide a valuable record of the island life that the whaler saw. The female figure on the left is shown in an outfit that has become the cliché attire for island maidens—the grass skirt. The figure in the center has a long gun casually slung over his shoulder and a spear in his right hand. The firearm was almost certainly "trade goods." The shape of the spear suggests that it may have been a whaler's lance. The hunter is wearing graphically patterned tapa, or bark cloth. The reverse side of the tooth on the right shows more of the local flora as well as young dancers.

SPERM-WHALE TOOTH WITH PATRIOTIC MOTIF, TWO VIEWS

Nantucket Whaling Museum

The scrimshander frequently chose to work a tooth in a horizontal aspect on one side and vertical on the other. Here, in the horizontal, is an American whaleship under full sail. The opposite side shows an oval cameo of the flag of Liberty being planted. Above are draped flags and the artist's rendition of the U.S. Seal.

There have been many modifications to the "Seal" since its adoption by the Founding Fathers. The Great Seal and the Seal of the President of the United States each have their unique design specifications.

President Harry S. Truman in 1945 signed an Executive Order that modified the design of the Presidential Seal. The olive branch (of peace) would be clutched in the eagle's right talon, and the eagle's head would face in that direction.

SPERM-WHALE TEETH WITH PATRIOTIC THEME
Nantucket Whaling Museum

The American sailor on the left strikes a jaunty pose as he waves his flat-brimmed hat, his hair blowing in the breeze. Accurate indications of a sailor's attire can be gained from scrimshaw like this. He is shown with bell-bottomed pants with a buttoned fly that is similar to the thirteen-button flap that is familiar to the U.S. Navy. He has a loose blouse, black kerchief or neck scarf, and short fitted coat. The circle of stars on the polychrome flag indicates that the nation was still quite young. The eagle behind him holds a banner that says FREE TRADE AND SAILOR'S RIGHTS. England frequently harassed American vessels and often "pressed" men—forced them to join the crew of the English warship.

    The female figure on the right shares the nautical theme. She, too, leans against an anchor. She and the eagle are holding a banner saying VIRTUE—LIBERTY AND INDEPENDENCE. Both designs are rich with cross-hatching, which gives weight and texture to the images.

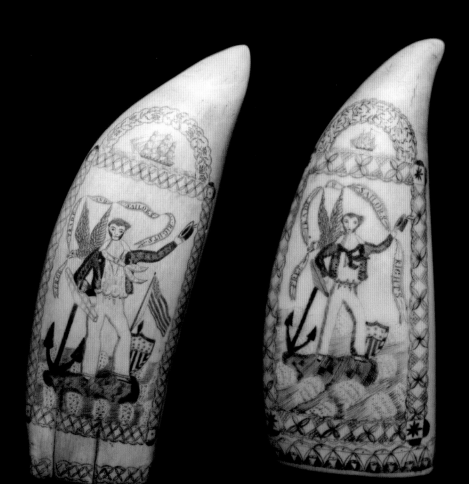

BOOK ILLUSTRATION, PORTRAIT
John F. Kennedy: Scrimshaw Collector, *by Clare Barnes, Jr.*

Shortly after Massachusetts senator John Fitzgerald Kennedy was elected president and took office, he was given the tooth shown here, engraved with the president's image, as a gift from the city of Fairhaven, Massachusetts. Milton Delano, the man who had decorated the ivory tooth, personally presented it to the president. The presentation took place on the tarmac of what was then Otis Air Force Base on Cape Cod.

BOOK ILLUSTRATION, SPERM-WHALE TOOTH WITH PRESIDENTIAL SEAL
John F. Kennedy: Scrimshaw Collector, *by Clare Barnes, Jr.*

As the 1964 book points out, John Kennedy was an astute collector of scrimshaw. Over twenty pieces decorated the desk and shelves of the Oval Office.

The First Lady, Jacqueline, commissioned Milton Delano to create the work shown here—a giant sperm-whale tooth decorated with the Presidential Seal. It was her surprise gift to her husband on Christmas morning in 1962. Less than a year later she would place the item he treasured into his coffin, just before his burial.

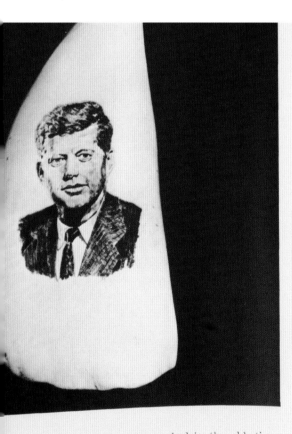

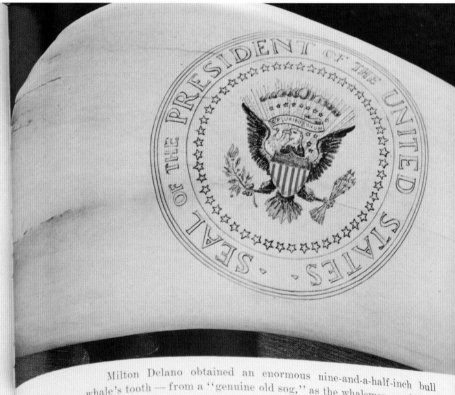

of the few living men who worked in the old, time-
itional way of scrimshawing. Kennedy was delighted
expressed his high admiration for Mr. Delano's ability
artist.

rk on the portrait tooth led to Mrs. Kennedy's request
w the Seal of the President of the United States on a

l described the device on the Presidential Seal to make
nual Message to Congress on the State of the Union,
1. The President listed some of the problems fac-
ation, and, he continued:

Milton Delano obtained an enormous nine-and-a-half-inch bull whale's tooth — from a "genuine old sog," as the whalemen would say — that had been brought to New Bedford in the year 1818. He spent two hundred and forty hours etching, coloring and polishing an ornate, early nineteenth century version of the Seal on the ancient ivory, changing only the number of stars in the border to fifty. The giant tooth was then mounted on a base of walnut taken from the captain's cabin of the old Dartmouth whaling bark *Sunbeam*. On a sparkling October day Delano delivered it to Mrs. Kennedy at the summer White House in Hyannis Port.

The President was absolutely enchanted with his present on Christmas morning in 1962. He treasured it not only as a beautiful work of scrimshaw, but for the thoughtful and loving interest that prompted the gift. From that day, the huge tooth held the place of honor on th

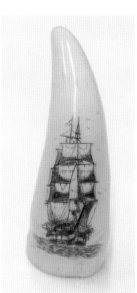

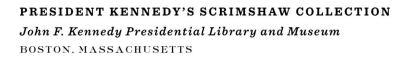

PRESIDENT KENNEDY'S SCRIMSHAW COLLECTION
John F. Kennedy Presidential Library and Museum
BOSTON, MASSACHUSETTS

This is part of the collection that President Kennedy kept on display in the Oval Office. He was a very serious and thoughtful collector. His collection has only a few depictions of whaling life. He favored heroic naval ships, America's founding fathers and early Boston scenes that reminded him of his old political district—Bunker Hill.

FIVE TEETH DECORATED WITH PATRIOTIC MOTIF, TWO VIEWS
Nantucket Whaling Museum

The large teeth at each end are polychromed to render the flag colors. All use a blue ink (and a style) that suggests tattoo art.

The reverse of each tooth, shown below, is sparsely decorated to play up the distinctive five-pointed stars.

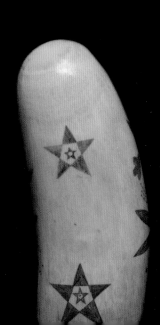

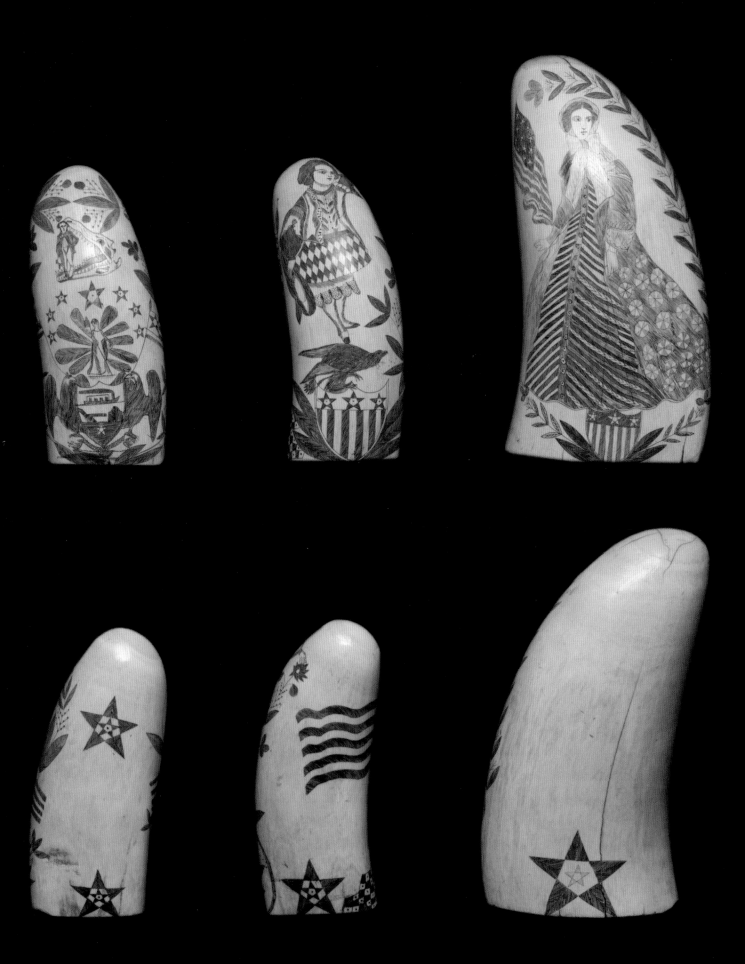

SEALSKIN MITTENS

Martha's Vineyard Museum

Like the snow goggles, mittens such as these could have been examples of whalemen adopting "local knowledge" to keep warm in extreme weather. This pair seems to have seen little use. They show off fine craftsmanship and design sense.

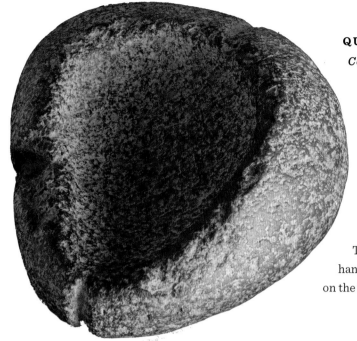

QUILLIQ—INUIT BLUBBER LAMP
Cold Spring Harbor Whaling Museum

Yankee whalemen developed a working relationship
with the native Inuit in the far north. This hollowed
stone is a rather small example of a quilliq, which
usually burned seal blubber. The blubber was
chewed or pounded to a macerated consistency
and a wick of moss or cotton fluff was put along one
edge and lit. The quilliq provided a good bit of light
as well as heat in a tightly built snow or ice house.
The three grooves along the sides may have been for a
hanging sling. The quilliq stone got quite hot, so if it was
on the icy floor it would be propped up on pegs.

FRAMED BENJAMIN FRANKLIN PORTRAIT
Nantucket Whaling Museum

Benjamin Franklin's mother, Abiah Folger, was born on Nantucket.
While Benjamin was born in Boston and is closely associated
with Philadelphia, throughout his busy life he maintained
family ties to the island.

Franklin was curious about the fact that English
merchant and packet ships took an average of two weeks
longer to cross to America compared with Yankee vessels.
He broached the subject with his cousin Timothy Folger,
a Nantucket whaling captain, who explained that the
Americans knew to compensate for powerful mid-ocean
currents. These currents were well known to mariners
going back to the 1500s. In fact, whales were known to feed
at the perimeters of this strong, predictable flow.

Franklin persuaded Captain Folger and many of his fellow
captains to keep records detailing water temperature, seasonal
variation in direction of flow and other pertinent data. In 1770
Benjamin Franklin published the first comprehensive nautical chart
of the phenomenon, which he named the "Gulf Stream."

NANTUCKET QUAKER HEADWEAR—THREE GENTLEMAN'S HATS, ONE LADY'S BONNET
Nantucket Whaling Museum

The Society of Friends (Quakers) would take a dim view of one of their own dressing extravagantly. Even those who had acquired the means to costume themselves splendidly would be reminded that bright colors and vain attachment to the latest fashions were to be avoided. Still, whalers traveled the world, saw how others dressed and realized the importance of communicating their status by the clothes that they wore.

The lady's bonnet with its bland homespun color and face-hiding brim still subtly hints at femininity. As schisms developed among the Quakers, the shape of a lady's bonnet could sometimes identify her sect.

The gentleman's hat to the left of the bonnet would have been more crisply blocked, with the brim smartly curled.

1838 SOCIETY OF FRIENDS MEETING HOUSE
Fair Street, Nantucket

The community on Nantucket grew from its beginnings with just a few families into a bustling whaling center of international renown. The influence and importance of Quakers on the island can be seen from the well-kept records recounting the construction, destruction and reconstruction of places of worship (meeting houses) on the island over the years.

This rather small structure with its "12 over 12" window panes and hipped roof was erected in 1838. By then, Nantucket's domination of the whale fishery was beginning to wane.

REVOLVING OPTIC (LENS) FROM SANKATY LIGHTHOUSE
Nantucket Whaling Museum

This device, originally lit by sperm whale oil, intensified (brightened) the flames from its three burning wicks into a powerful beam of light that could be seen 19 miles out into the Atlantic Ocean. It consumed 17.5 ounces of oil per hour. The combined weight of all the glass components is 3,530 pounds. The entire device revolved thanks to a system of weights and cables which needed to be frequently wound, like a clock. This was but one of the many tasks performed by the lighthouse keeper, who was known as the "wickie." Keeping the wicks trimmed and clean was another of his daily tasks.

It is technically a "2nd Order Fresnel Optic." Augustin-Jean Fresnel (pronounced Freh-NEL) was a great physicist and experimenter with light waves, who in 1821 invented the "lenticular apparatus" that bears his name. This beautifully preserved example was purchased in France and was first lit on Nantucket on February 1, 1850. Its effectiveness in warning ships of the dangerous reefs east of Nantucket was immediately seen. Local fishermen called it the "blazing star."

BIBLIOGRAPHY

Ackerman, Diane. *The Moon by Whale Light*. New York: Vintage, 1991.

Andersen, Harald T. *The Biology of Marine Mammals*. New York: Academic Press, 1969.

Ansel, Willits D. *The Whaleboat*. Mystic, CT: Mystic Seaport Museum, 1978.

Ardrey, Robert. *The Hunting Hypothesis*. New York: Atheneum, 1976.

Ashley, Clifford W. *The Yankee Whaler*. Garden City, NY: Halcyon, 1942.

Barbour, John A. *In the Wake of the Whale*. New York: Macmillan, 1969.

Barnes, Clare, Jr. *John F. Kennedy: Scrimshaw Collector*. Boston: Little, Brown, 1964.

Bjorgvinsson, Asbjorn, and Helmut Lugmayr. *Whale Watching in Iceland*. Reykjavik: JPV Publishers, 2002.

Bullen, Frank T. *The Cruise of the Cachalot*. Santa Barbara, CA: Narrative Press, 2001.

Chamberlain, Samuel. *Nantucket*. New York: Hastings House, 1955.

Chapelle, Howard I. *The American Fishing Schooners*. New York: W. W. Norton, 1973.

———. *Boatbuilding*. New York: W. W. Norton, 1941.

Cherfas, Jeremy. *The Hunting of the Whale*. London: Penguin, 1989.

Cone, Laurence. *For Candlesticks and Corset Stays: Long Island's Yankee Whalers*. Cold Spring Harbor, NY: Whaling Museum Society, 2007.

Craig, Adam Weir. *Whales and the Nantucket Whaling Museum*. Nantucket, MA: Nantucket Historical Association, 1977.

Culver, Henry B. *The Book of Old Ships*. Garden City, NY: Doubleday, Page & Co., 1924.

Daugherty, Anita E. *Marine Mammals of California*. Sacramento: California Department of Fish and Game, 1979.

Dolin, Eric Jay. *Leviathan*. New York, NY: W. W. Norton, 2007.

Drucker, Philip. *Indians of the Northwest Coast*. New York: American Museum of Natural History, McGraw-Hill, 1955.

Druett, Joan. *In the Wake of Madness*. Chapel Hill, NC: Algonquin Books of Chapel Hill, 2004.

Ellis, Richard. *Men and Whales*. New York: Knopf, 1991.

Flotsam and Jetsam. Savannah: Ships of the Sea Maritime Museum, 1998.

Fraser, F. C. *British Whales, Dolphins and Porpoises*. London: British Museum, 1976.

Gardner, Will. *The Coffin Saga: Nantucket's Story—From Settlement to Summer Visitors*. Nantucket, MA: Whaling Museum Publications, 1949.

Garner, Stanton, ed. *The Captain's Best Mate: The Journal of Mary Chipman Lawrence on the Whaler* Addison. Hanover, NH: University Press of New England, 1966.

Haley, Nelson Cole. *Whale Hunt: The Narrative of a Voyage*. Mystic, CT: Mystic Seaport Museum, 2002.

Hayden, Sterling. *Wanderer*. New York: Knopf, 1963.

Heller, Peter. *The Whale Warriors*. New York: Free Press, 2007.

Hill, David O. *Vanishing Giants: The History, Biology and Fate of the Great Whales*. New York: National Audubon Society, 1975.

Hoare, Philip. *The Whale: In Search of the Giants of the Sea*. London: Fourth Estate/ HarperCollins, 2008.

Hohman, Elmo Paul. *The American Whaleman*. New York: Longmans, Green & Co., 1928.

Humane Society of the United States. *The Case Against Marine Mammals in Captivity*. Washington, DC: Humane Society of the United States, 1995.

Jeune, Paul. *The Whale Who Wouldn't Die*. Chicago: Follett Publishing Co., 1979.

Kent, Rockwell. *N by E*. Hanover, NH: University Press of New England, 1996 (orig. 1930).

Kittredge, Henry C. *The Mooncussers of Cape Cod*. Boston: Houghton Mifflin, 1937.

Lawrence, Martha. *Scrimshaw: The Whaler's Legacy*. Atglen, PA: Schiffer Publishing, 1993.

Leach, Robert J., and Peter Gow. *Quaker Nantucket*. Nantucket, MA: Mill Hill Press, 1997.

Lytle, Thomas G. *Harpoons and Other Whalecraft*. New Bedford, MA: Old Dartmouth Historical Society, 1984.

Macy, Obed. *The History of Nantucket*. Boston: Hilliard Gray & Co., 1835.

Mays, Victor. *Fast Iron*. Boston: Houghton Mifflin, 1953.

McCullough, David. *John Adams*. New York: Simon & Schuster, 2001.

Melville, Herman. *Billy Budd*. London: Constable & Co., 1924.

———. *Moby-Dick; or, The Whale*. New York: Harper & Brothers, 1851.

———. *Redburn: His First Voyage*. New York: Harper & Brothers, 1849.

Mitchell, Edward. *Porpoise, Dolphin and Small Whale Fisheries of the World:*

Status and Problems. Morges, Switz.: International Union for the Conservation of Nature and Natural Resources, 1975.

Morell, Virginia. *Animal Wise: The Thoughts and Emotions of Our Fellow Creatures*. New York: Crown, 2013.

Morison, Samuel Eliot. *The Maritime History of Massachusetts*. Boston: Houghton Mifflin, 1921.

———. *The Ropemakers of Plymouth: A History of the Plymouth Cordage Company*. Cambridge, MA: Riverside Press, 1950.

Mowat, Farley. *A Whale for the Killing*. Boston: Little, Brown, 1972.

Murphy, Robert Cushman. *A Dead Whale or a Stove Boat*. Boston: Houghton Mifflin, 1967.

———. *Logbook for Grace*. New York: Macmillan, 1947.

Nichols, Daphne. *Lord Howe Island Rising*. Brookvale, Austral.: BA Printing & Publishing Services, 2006.

Nordhoff, Charles. *Whaling and Fishing*. New York: Dodd, Mead, 1895.

Olmsted, Francis Allyn. *Incidents of a Whaling Voyage*. New York, D. Appleton & Co., 1841.

Oppel, Frank, comp. *Tales of the New England Coast*. Edison, NJ: Castle Books, 1985.

Palmer, William R. *The Whaling Port of Sag Harbor*. Sag Harbor, NY: Sag Harbor Whaling Museum, 1959.

Philbrick, Nathaniel. *Away Off Shore: Nantucket Island and Its People 1602–1890*. New York: Penguin, 1984.

———. *In the Heart of the Sea: The Tragedy of the Whaleship* Essex. New York: Viking, 2001.

———. *Sea of Glory*. New York: Viking Penguin, 2003.

Robertson, R. B. *Of Whales and Men*. New York: Knopf, 1954.

Roscoe, Lee Stephanie. *Dreaming Monomoy's Past: Walking Its Present*. Brewster, MA: Woodlee Outlaw Press, 1965.

Sanderson, Ivan T. *Follow the Whale*. New York: Bramhall House, 1956.

Sapir, Edward, et al. *Legendary Hunters: The Whaling Indians*. Ethnology Paper 139. Ottawa: Canadian Museum of Civilization, 2004.

Scheffer, Victor B. *The Year of the Whale*. New York: Scribner's, 1969.

Stackpole, Edouard A. *The Sea Hunters: The New England Whalemen During Two Centuries, 1635–1835*. Philadelphia: J. B. Lippincott Co., 1953.

———, and Peter H. Dryer. *Nantucket in Color*. New York: Hastings House, 1973.

Starbuck, Alexander. *History of the American Whale Fishery*. Secaucus, NJ: Castle Books, 1989.

Van Doren, Carl. *Benjamin Franklin*. New York: Viking, 1938.

Verrill, A. Hyatt. *The Real Story of the Whaler: Whaling, Past and Present*. New York: D. Appleton & Co., 1922.

The Whaling Question: The Inquiry by Sir Sydney Frost of Australia. San Francisco: Friends of the Earth, 1979.

Whipple, A. B. C. *Yankee Whalers in the South Seas.* Rutland, VT: Charles E. Tuttle & Co., 1973.

Whitehead, Hal. *Sperm Whales: Social Evolution in the Ocean.* Chicago: University of Chicago Press, 2003.

Williams, Heathcote. *Whale Nation.* New York: Harmony Books, 1988.

Williams, Winston. *Nantucket Then and Now.* New York: Dodd, Mead, 1977.

Winn, Lois King, and Howard E. Winn. *Wings in the Sea: The Humpback Whale.* Hanover, NH: University Press of New England, 1985.

Wynne, Kate. *Guide to Marine Mammals of Alaska.* Fairbanks: University of Alaska Fairbanks, 2007.

Zacks, Richard. *The Pirate Hunter.* New York: Hyperion Books, 2002.